An Introduction to Personal Finance

(A Republic of Ireland/ United Kingdom text)

Published in 2008 by
Institute of Chartered Accountants in Ireland
Burlington House, Burlington Road
Dublin 4

ISBN: 978-0-903854-48-1

An Introduction to Personal Finance

(A Republic of Ireland/ United Kingdom text)

First Edition

Anne Marie Ward

(BA (hons), Macc, FCA, PGCUT, PhD, FHEA)
School of Accounting, University of
Ulster at Jordanstown

THE INSTITUTE OF
Chartered Accountants
IN IRELAND

LIABILITY

At the outset it his highlighted that the author is NOT a financial adviser. This book and its contents should not be taken as financial advice. Each and every individual is different, their circumstances, needs, objectives, etc., are different. Independent financial advice should always be obtained from an appropriately qualified registered financial adviser. It is a criminal offence to provide financial advice, if not registered with the appropriate regulatory body.

For mum and dad

ABBREVIATED CONTENTS

DETAILED CONTENTS

ACKNOWLEDGEMENTS

Martin McKee, my husband, is top of the acknowledgement list. I thank him for rearing our children, whilst I spend most of my time at the computer. I also thank him for proof reading this book and for his general support.

Thanks also to the reviewers, the typesetters (Hurix), the copy editor (Barrett Business Communications) and Agnieszka Pobedynska (ICAI publishing department) for her efficient handling of the whole publication process. Special thanks go to Barry Quinn, a qualified independent financial adviser, for his review and helpful suggestions.

PREFACE

When an individual has a strong awareness of their ability to generate funds, has knowledge of their expenditure and debt commitments (and the associated cost of this debt), has formalised their financial objectives, considered their financial responsibility for dependents and evaluated their retirement needs, then they are in a strong position to have financial control over their lives. Having financial control means not being financially dependent on relatives and/or the government. By preparing a financial plan, individuals can carefully manage their income and expenditure, can identify their financial risk and take steps to minimise it, can target bad expensive debt for clearance, can highlight good investment opportunities that match their risk-return profile, can start to provide for their retirement and in general, increase their net worth in the most tax efficient manner. Many individuals, particularly those with business qualifications or business experience, do follow good personal financial practices - other people are maybe not as aware of the consequences of poor financial planning.

This text tries to shed some light on the financial planning process, by highlighting information that a typical financial adviser might gather before providing financial advice. It also considers possible influences on advice given. There are four key areas that have to be considered in light of the all the background information and influences; risk management, debt management, investment management and retirement planning. Having an understanding of the time value of money is also important for personal financial planning. In general, it is recommended that younger people (who have the greatest capital rationing problems) should be the most frugal and should even at this early stage, be thinking about their retirement needs. Responsibility for the encouragement of good financial practices should be championed by parents, educators and employers.

A brief simple explanation is provided in this text of the main types of investment product that an individual may find themselves investing in, either directly or through their pension. The most important issue to consider is the risk exposure of the various investments to external influences, such as the condition of the economy. It is highlighted that a diversified portfolio of negatively correlated investments is the best investment option and individuals with higher net worth are in a stronger position to obtain this type of portfolio as they can afford property, equity and bonds.

Pensions are reasonably complex: there are several types (public, private, occupational) and each has different rules and tax breaks. A brief synopsis of each type is given in this text, though readers should obtain more detailed information on the different types of pension from their financial adviser before investing in one. It is noted that the government policy in the Republic of Ireland (ROI) is more generous towards retired people, than the policy available to retired people in the United Kingdom (UK).

PEDAGOGY

Learning objectives: In each chapter the expected competencies to be gained by readers are outlined at the outset.

Chapter clarity: Each chapter begins with an introduction which explains the flow and connection between topics included in the chapter. The body of each chapter provides detail and a conclusion sums up, by highlighting key points.

Worked examples: The worked examples increase in complexity as a chapter progresses.

Key terms: When key terms are first defined in a chapter they are highlighted in ***bold and italicised***. At the end of each chapter the key terms are summarised in a table. The reader should be aware of the key terms and should revisit the chapter when unable to define/explain the key term.

Websites: When relevant, lists of websites that can be visited by readers are provided.

Review questions: These questions are designed to assist readers in identifying and revising the key issues within each chapter. It is a way for readers to provide themselves with feedback on their understanding of each topic. Solutions are provided in Appendix 3. The questions range from short quick-fire questions, to examination standard questions. Successful completion of the more challenging questions demonstrates a thorough understanding of the issues covered in the chapter and indeed may refer to issues covered in preceding chapters.

Mathematics made simple: This text does not try to derive mathematical formula, or to prove existing accepted models. In each instance the accepted approach is explained in simple terms using narrative. A formula is provided and an example of how to calculate the outcome of the formula using input variables is given.

Index tables: Index tables have been provided in the appendices to save readers time when they are adjusting cash flows for the time value of money.

Abbreviations: A list of abbreviations used in the text has been provided, for quick reference for readers.

Bibliography: The readers of this text can deepen their understanding of areas of interest to them by sourcing the work of other authors. The bibliography contains text books, newspapers articles and academic literature that are considered relevant by the writer.

CHAPTER 1

INTRODUCTION

LEARNING OBJECTIVES

This chapter provides a brief overview of this text.

AIM OF TEXT AND OVERVIEW OF EACH CHAPTER

This book serves to cover the main issues of personal financial management at an introductory level. Personal financial planning can be considered to focus on six areas: current lifestyle, risk management, debt, savings, investments and retirement planning (pensions).

Before the main personal finance decisions are covered, chapter two, 'Political and Economic Influences on Financial Planning', provides some background on political and economic influences on an individual's financial situation. This chapter discusses the impact of changes in the government's pension policy, stock market performance and changes in interest rates on an individual's financial position. This helps to highlight the growing importance of personal financial planning and provides an awareness of the growing risk to which individuals' finances are exposed.

In chapter three, the preparation of a financial plan for an individual is dealt with. This chapter is written from the perspective of the preparer of the financial plan being different to the individual being assessed. By assuming that the plan is being prepared for a different individual, the reader is made more aware of the process and the underlying factors that impact on a financial plan. In this text, the preparation of a financial plan has been broken into nine steps including — determining the profile of the individual, identifying financial issues, assessing the individual's risk attitude, setting objectives for the individual, identifying the current financial position and earnings potential of the individual, preparing a financial plan for the individual, reviewing the financial plan and updating it to take account of changes in the individual's situation. Most financial advisers will prepare a variety of financial plans for an individual, reflecting different scenarios. A financial plan is only as good as the information it contains. This information is sourced from the individual, so the onus is on an individual to provide relevant, reliable and realistic estimates of cash flows expected and valuations for assets held and debts owed. The plan will only be of benefit to an individual if they heed the advice given by the financial adviser and stick to the projected plan.

Chapter four, 'The Financial Lifecycle', considers factors that are deemed to be most important to an individual at different stages of their life cycle. No two financial plans will be the same. Every individual is different. However, there are common issues that face most individuals as they progress through life. This chapter splits peoples' lives into periods, or stages, which are aligned with age and highlights the main issues that affect individuals within these periods. The stages include students, young employed individuals, individuals who have dependents, established individuals and retired individuals.

Chapter five, 'Insurance' introduces one of the first decision factors that an individual has to consider. Insurance reduces risk and an individual has to decide whether they are going to pay to reduce risk, or not. It is generally advised that individuals, as a minimum, protect their income and take steps to cover a potential critical illness. The amount of insurance taken depends on an individual's attitude to risk and on their personal circumstances. For example, a young, healthy individual with no partner or dependents is likely to opt for less insurance cover than a married individual who has children. If an individual is unable to build up savings and investments then they are exposed to more risk and are more likely to opt for more insurance cover. This chapter describes the most common products used by individuals — family income benefit, permanent health insurance, critical illness, a variety of life assurance products, private medical insurance and payment protection insurance.

Debt management requires particular attention in an individual's early years. If debt is not controlled from the outset, it can hinder an individual's ability to become financially self-sufficient. Chapter six, 'Debt Management', considers the different types of debt, differentiating between what is regarded as 'good debt', and 'bad debt', highlights pitfalls that can cause a person to end up in financial difficulty and suggests steps to take to manage personal debt.

Two of the main decisions facing an individual throughout their life — determining the level of funds to invest and selecting the correct investment — are covered in chapters seven, 'Savings' and chapter eight, 'Investments'. Chapter seven considers the purpose of having savings, provides tips on good savings practices and summarises briefly the main savings products that are available in the UK and in the ROI. Chapter eight, 'Investments', outlines the relationship between risk, inflation, debt and liquidity on individuals' investment policies and describes, in brief, the main investment products used in personal finance. This chapter provides more detail on investment in property relative to other investment products, as this type of investment has become more popular with private individuals over the past three decades

The different types of pension are discussed in chapter nine, 'Pensions' for both the ROI and the UK and finally in chapter ten the regulation of the financial services markets in both jurisdictions is explained.

CHAPTER 2

POLITICAL AND ECONOMIC INFLUENCES ON FINANCIAL PLANNING

LEARNING OBJECTIVES

Upon completion of this chapter, readers should be able to:

- Explain the meaning of the key terms listed at the end of the chapter;
- Outline the principles of personal financial management
- Explain the benefits of good financial planning;
- Describe changes in policy that have resulted in more uncertainty for individuals' financial security; and
- Explain the impact of economic changes on individuals' financial security.

FINANCIAL PLANNING

Good *financial planning* strives to provide individuals with the ability to meet their personal financial aspirations both now and in the future. Good financial planning should lead to social and economic benefits for an individual. It should increase the ability of an individual to be able to be *financially self-sufficient*, to feel financially secure and to ensure that sufficient steps are taken so that this remains the case throughout the entire life of the individual (including when retired). The importance of having strong personal finance has increased over the past 30 years because of changes in policy and an increase in the exposure of individuals' finances to economic risk.

PERSONAL FINANCE AND GOVERNMENT WELFARE

At one time an individual could feel secure about their financial future if they were paying into a pension, both at work and with their 'stamp'. This, they believed, was sufficient to take care of them when they retired. However, this is no longer the case. The governments in the ROI and in the UK operate a *'pay-as-you-go'* policy, paying current pensions out of current employee tax (there is no pension's pot!). This problem is exasperated by the shift in the age demographics of the population. People are living longer now than when the welfare state was first introduced. In addition, the pension age has fallen and the standard of living expected by pensioners has risen.

Indeed the standard of welfare expected by the general public, from the government (both in the ROI and in the UK), has increased dramatically over the past 30 years. For example, the proportion of school leavers attending university has increased significantly, the care expected from the National Health Service has increased significantly and children have to stay in school to 16 years of age (at one time this was 14) and this is mooted to increase to 18 in the coming years. In addition, providing housing for those with no income/low income has increased significantly.

The result is that governments find it difficult to service the pension demands of current pensioners from taxes raised from the tax-paying portion of the population. Therefore, changes have been occurring to the welfare system since the late 1970s. *Private funding* has been creeping its way into the welfare system, with many individuals now having their own private health insurance, having to pay for university education (Northern Ireland (NI), England and Wales) and having to pay for dental treatment (these services were free in the UK). Indeed, the government is trying to shift the responsibility for providing for individuals (when retired) back on to individuals, by introducing incentives to get people to cater for their retirement. For example, in NI, Individual Savings Accounts (ISAs) are available and in the ROI, a similar product, the Special Savings Incentive Accounts (SSIAs) had been championed by the government. SSIAs are no longer available, but Personal Retirement Savings Accounts (PRSAs) are. These products are afforded generous tax breaks. They were established with the aim of encouraging individuals to save regularly and to lock funds away for a number of years. In addition to these savings products, in both jurisdictions, tax breaks are also available for contributions to private pension schemes. This is discussed in detail in chapter nine, 'Pensions'.

The UK Government also changed the way state pensions for employed individuals, who pay extra national insurance contributions, are calculated. At one time when an individual paid national insurance contributions over a certain level, they were entitled to a second pension. The level of this second pension was related to the level of additional national insurance contributions paid. This is no longer the case. Now the government has placed a floor (which benefits low-income individuals) and a cap on the pension that can be received by high-earning individuals. Moreover, most benefits are now means tested.

The result of the changes in government policy is that there is greater requirement for individuals, particularly those who are high earners and who want to sustain their quality of life for the rest of their lives, to take more responsibility for their own financial destiny.

PERSONAL FINANCE AND THE MARKETS

Further complications to face individuals when they undertake financial planning are the risks associated with equity investments. Pension companies invest heavily in the equity stock markets and the value of an individual's pension will be affected by movements in the value of shares quoted on stock markets.

The impact of the global stock markets' decline on the value of company pension schemes in the 1990s meant that many individuals, who retired in this period, found that their private pension was not what they had anticipated. Indeed, the volatility of stock markets, and the collapse of some major companies and professional entities (such as UK Equitable Life, Enron, WorldCom, Arthur Andersen) reduced public confidence in private and occupational pension schemes. The consequence is that individuals cannot rely on their pension as the only form of investment to cater for their retirement, so they have to take responsibility for their own finances if they want to be financially self-sufficient.

PERSONAL FINANCE AND THE CREDIT CRUNCH

The financial problems facing most individuals are exasperated by the current debt culture. The use of credit was promoted by the Thatcher Government in the 1980s when they deregulated the financial markets, opening up the UK to foreign competition, resulting in low-cost debt, which was easier to obtain (similar deregulatory changes happened in Ireland). Having debt increases an individual's risk exposure to changes in interest rates. In 2006 and 2007 there were six one-quarter percent increases in interest rates in the UK, increasing the bank base rate from 4.5% in July 2006 to 5.75% in July 2007. A similar pattern of interest rate increases occurred in the ROI as the European Central Bank increased its base rate from 2.5% in March 2006 to 4% by March 2007. In both regions, the interest rate increases (combined with the deterioration in the sub-prime lending market in the US) caused a slowdown in the economy, a fall in consumer confidence and spending, a reduction in house prices and an increase in bankruptcy cases, mortgage arrears and house repossessions.

The result nearly spelt disaster for one large financial institution based in London — Northern Rock Bank. This bank experienced a run on their accounts, as customers withdrew their savings, worried about the level of mortgage arrears and bad debts being experienced by the bank. The Northern Rock received assistance (about £55 billion) by way of an inter-bank loan from the central Bank of England and the UK Government, and in February 2008 the UK Government ended up nationalising the bank, after months of negotiations with a number of interested takeover parties, including Richard Branson, and the internal management team. The UK Government felt that this was the only option open to them as so much of the public's funds had been invested.

To alleviate the problems facing the slowing economy in the UK, the Bank of England reduced interest rates by one-quarter of a percent in December 2007 and by a further one-quarter of a percent in February 2008. The Bank of England base rate is currently 5% (August 2008).

The European Central Bank kept its base rate unchanged since June 2007 and a year later the rate remained at 4%.

Though the increasing interest rates that occurred in both jurisdictions in 2006 and 2007 might be considered to have impacted greatly on individuals and the economy, the one-and-a-half percent increase over the nine-month period in the UK (bringing the base rate up to 5.75%) is minor relative to the rate increases that incurred on 16 September 1992, when the Conservative Government (under the leadership of Sir John Major) hiked base rates from an already high 10% to 15%, though they settled at 12% by the end of the day.

Most people in today's society have debt, and are exposed to risk from the impact of interest rate increases on their disposable income. Therefore, there is a need for individuals to manage personal finance appropriately. This process should involve considering, in advance, the impact of changes in interest rates on their disposable income, before committing to debt.

PERSONAL FINANCE AND INFLATION

Over the latter half of 2007 and in 2008 (to date) individuals have also experienced, at first hand, just how vulnerable their disposable income is to inflation. The soaring cost of energy (oil, electricity, coal and gas) has had the knock-on effect of making virtually every product an individual purchases more expensive. In most instances this has reduced disposable income. This is particularly significant to individuals who have high levels of debt as governments usually use interest rate increases to curb inflation. In addition, debt repayments are not-negotiable — they are a fixed cash outflow. These individuals may find themselves in financial difficulties. Good financial planning would always strive to ensure that individuals do not leave themselves exposed to such an extent that it causes financial difficulties.

KEY TERMS

Financial planning   Pay-as-you-go
Financially self-sufficient   Private funding

REVIEW QUESTIONS

(Answers to review questions are provided in Appendix three)

1. What changes in government policy have occurred that have resulted in a greater need for individuals to take control of their own financial destiny?
2. How do changes in interest rates impact on private individuals' personal wealth?
3. How has the surge in oil prices impacted on private individuals' wealth?
4. List two initiatives that the government in your jurisdiction has undertaken to encourage individuals to put funds away for their retirement.

CHAPTER 3

THE FINANCIAL PLAN

LEARNING OBJECTIVES

Upon completion of this chapter, readers should be able to:

- Explain the meaning of the key terms listed at the end of the chapter;
- List the nine stages to a financial plan;
- Detail the background information required about an individual before preparing a financial plan;
- Describe financial issues that individuals face that need to be considered before preparing a financial plan;
- Prepare a schedule to determine an individual's risk attitude;
- Determine the goals and objectives of an individual for the purpose of preparing a financial plan;
- Calculate the net worth of an individual;
- Prepare a personal cash budget based on an individual's current details;
- Prepare projections, taking into account various scenarios; and
- Detail how the plan should be monitored in the future.

INTRODUCTION: THE FINANCIAL PLAN

A *financial plan* consolidates information about an individual (and their partner) in one document. It summarises their financial aims and aspirations and formalises how these can be financed. When preparing a financial plan the same decision-making principles that are applied in business finance and management accounting in companies can be applied. Most decisions go through the process of planning, implementation and control. This is the same for decision-making in personal finance. Companies set their objectives and make decisions in light of these objectives. Individuals should do the same. There are also similarities between the major decisions that a company faces and those that individuals should consider. In companies the main decisions are categorised as the investment, finance and dividend decisions. In personal finance the decisions include the investment decision (savings, personal investments and pensions) and the finance decision (debt). These decisions are influenced by an individual's choice of lifestyle, attitude to risk, their income, expenditure, health, financial commitments and dependents. All of the decisions are interrelated. For example, if a person elects to have an extravagant lifestyle now, then the level of investment will be lower and debt may be higher. This may have long-term financial consequences. However, the individual may feel that it is worth it. An example here may be parents who give up work to look after young children. A conscious decision is made to forgo income in return for quality of life. So long as individuals are aware of the impact of their decisions now, on their future, this is not an issue.

The process of preparing a financial plan can be split into nine steps. The steps are outlined in the following diagram:

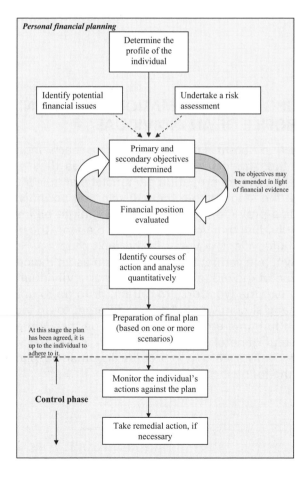

The first three stages identified in the diagram are concerned with obtaining background knowledge of the individual. Every individual is different and it is important to prepare a financial plan that is tailored to suit the individual. The next four stages (setting objectives, obtaining financial information, gathering information about and selecting a course of action, preparing the financial plan) are more concrete – they formalise a course of action to be taken by the individual to achieve their financial objectives. The final two steps are concerned with monitoring and control. Each of the stages is now considered in more depth. The financial plan can be prepared for the individual on their own, or may include information on their partner also.

BACKGROUND INFORMATION: DETERMINING THE PROFILE OF AN INDIVIDUAL

There are different financial stages to each individual's life and their financial goals will change as they progress through life. Before preparing a financial plan it is important to gauge the stage within the lifecycle that an individual is at. Age is a proxy for determining what might be important to the individual that you are trying to plan for (the personal financial lifecycle is covered in the next chapter). However, on its own, age cannot be fully relied on as an indicator of a stereotype of individual. For example, an individual in their 40s may exit the workforce to retrain, or to go to university. Their financial plan would be very different to an individual who is in full-time employment with a partner and dependents. Useful general information on an individual which is necessary before starting to prepare any financial plan might include the following:

General information on the profile of the individual/family

	Self	*Partner*
Surname:	_____	_____
Christian name:	_____	_____
Date of birth:	_____	_____
Occupation:	_____	_____
Telephone number (home):	_____	_____
Telephone number (work)	_____	_____
Mobile number:	_____	_____
Fax:	_____	_____
Email:	_____	_____
Home address:		
Correspondence address (if different to home address):		

Married *(Circle)*   Yes/No

BACKGROUND INFORMATION: IDENTIFYING POTENTIAL FINANCIAL ISSUES

It is important at this stage to analyse an individual's risks. *Risk* in financial planning is the chance that an individual's actual cash flows turn out to be different to what was predicted in the financial plan. Therefore an analysis of common factors that may impinge an individual's ability to generate cash flows in the future, or that may create cash outflows have to be considered at the outset. In particular, the plan should try to determine the expected lifespan of the individual. This will impact on savings, investment and pension requirements.

Risk to cash inflows

Health is a **critical risk factor**, which can have serious financial consequences. A person who does not smoke, take drugs or drink, has no family history of illnesses and who exercises regularly is likely to have a healthy, financially productive and long working life. Having this information strengthens the potential to make more accurate estimates of future earnings and life expectancy. This should be factored into the financial plan. If a person's health is not good and their life-expectancy is short, a different financial plan will result and different advice will be given. An example of health assessments being undertaken to assess risk in practice is experienced by every individual when they obtain a quote for an insurance product. In addition, health checklists and medical examinations now form part of most entities' recruitment process.

Influences on cash outflows

It is also important to identify **potential financial commitments**, such as having to finance dependants (children, or elderly parents). Most individuals are aware, from a young age, of their view on having children. Children are an expensive commitment and individuals who wish to raise children need to start thinking about 'nests' at an early stage. Children need to be financed for about 18 years. If a child is disabled, the term of care extends to the child's lifetime and a responsible parent needs to ensure that the child is catered for financially for the period of the child's life (which may extend beyond the parent's life). From an early stage in the financial lifecycle, individuals can start to plan for the cost of providing for their children in the future.

Caring for elderly parents is another issue. Individuals should consider what they are going to do about their parents, in their parent's later years. If they are going to take responsibility for the care of their parents, then the financial consequences need to be factored into the individual's financial plan. A proforma to capture this type of information might look something like the following:

General information on potential financial issues

Health:	Individual	Partner
Current health *(circle)*	Good/ok/poor	Good/ok/poor
Risk factors:		
Smoker *(circle)*	Yes/No	Yes/No
Drink alcohol beyond recommended levels *(circle)*	Yes/No	Yes/No
Other high risk factors *(discuss)*	Yes/No	Yes/No
Education:		
Do you have any children *(circle)*	Yes/No	Yes/No

If you have children who are dependent on you please provide the following details:

	Name	Date of birth	Years of education to finance	Expected yearly cost
Child 1			(N)	
			(P)	
			(S)	
			(U)	
Child 2			(N)	
			(P)	
			(S)	
			(U)	
Child 3			(N)	
			(P)	
			(S)	
			(U)	
Child 4			(N)	
			(P)	
			(S)	
			(U)	

Where (N) is Nursery school   (P) is Primary school
(S) is Secondary school   (U) is University

Details of other dependents who are relying on you for financial help *(include an estimate of the yearly commitment and when this cash outflow is expected to start; this may include grand-children or elderly parents)*

_____

_____

_____

BACKGROUND INFORMATION: UNDERTAKING A RISK ASSESSMENT

Getting information on an individual's attitude to **investment risk** and **earnings risk** is also important. Some individuals are risk takers, others are risk adverse. The financial plan should try to identify the risk profile of an individual at the outset. This will influence the financial plan and the financial advice given. An example of some questions that could be used to capture **investment risk** – the level of risk an individual wishes to expose their funds to – might include the following:

Possible questions to assess risk exposure

	Individual	Partner
Investment risk		
How long are you willing to lock funds away for? (This will depend on your future needs)	___Years	___Years
How much are you willing to lock away?	€/£___	€/£___
Do you require it to be accessible?	Yes/No	Yes/No
If you answered yes, identify the proportion?	_____%	_____%
Would you be happy to risk part of your capital investment in the chance that you may get a higher return (circle)?	Yes/No	Yes/No
If yes, what proportion?	_____%	_____%
If you answered yes to the previous question, can you tell me the level of risk you are willing to accept (circle).	High/medium/low	High/medium/low
Do you need the remaining protected capital investment to accumulate growth /earn a return which is above inflation?	Yes/No	Yes/No

An example of some questions that could be used to capture *earnings risk* – the potential for changes in income and the impact of changes in income on the financial plan – are as follows:

Possible questions to assess risk exposure (continued)

	Individual	Partner
Earnings potential risk		
Have you considered the impact on your finances of either of you passing away?	Yes/No	Yes/No
Circle importance	*Is this issue:* VeryImp/Imp/NotImp	*Is this issue:* VeryImp/Imp/NotImp
Have you considered the impact on your finances of either of you becoming incapacitated?	Yes/No	Yes/No
Circle importance	*Is this issue:* VeryImp/Imp/NotImp	*Is this issue:* VeryImp/Imp/NotImp
Have you considered the options available when you are elderly and in need of care?	Yes/No	Yes/No
Circle importance	*Is this issue:* VeryImp/Imp/NotImp	*Is this issue:* VeryImp/Imp/NotImp
Have you considered estate planning?	Yes/No	Yes/No
Circle importance	*Is this issue:* VeryImp/Imp/NotImp	*Is this issue:* VeryImp/Imp/NotImp

---

Once this background information has been collected and reviewed, the individual's financial aspirations for the future should be recorded.

DETERMINING THE GOALS OF THE INDIVIDUAL

Like in any financial decision-making process an individual's **primary objective** has to be determined at the outset.

This objective is a long-term strategic goal which will have a major impact on the individual's life. It is the ultimate goal and all actions should be taken with this objective in mind. An example might be the wish to build up sufficient funds to enable the individual's current lifestyle to be sustained when retired, or maybe to have a family and children, or own a house. The objective does not have to be financial, but it usually has financial implications – for example, having children in itself is a personal decision but has major financial consequences. Other *secondary objectives* should also be determined and ranked according to importance. Secondary objectives are not as important as the primary objective. These objectives might be short-term (buying a flash car, going on a skiing holiday, having laser hair removal), or long-term (obtaining a rental property, sending children to university, having a fund to pay for funeral expenses – personal planning involves being a little morbid!). It might be that there is conflict between objectives. In these instances the objectives which are more congruent with the primary objective should be selected. It may be that the individual has goals that are just not achievable given all the information provided.

Schedule to identify primary and secondary objectives (rank in order of importance)

Objectives	Example responses	More information
Primary		
Short-term	Purchase own home	Mortgage-free when retired.
Long-term	Financial security for the family	Have net income of €/£50,000 when retired/when partner dies/if disabled/if partner disabled, in today's terms.
Secondary		
Short-term	Finance children's education	Require a fund of approximately €/£50,000 for each child in today's terms.
	Be debt efficient/ intelligent	Reduce expensive bad debt. Reduce the financial pressure experienced each month.

(Continued)

Schedule to identify primary and secondary objectives (rank in order of importance) (continued)

Objectives Secondary	Example responses	More information
Short-term	Start saving/investing regularly	Analyse current income and expenditure and highlight potential savings to be made and investment opportunities.
Long-term	Start a financial fund for retirement	Linked to the primary objective.
	Purchase an investment property	Consider the local/overseas markets.
	Consider inheritance	Make a will/start a trust.

IDENTIFYING THE CURRENT FINANCIAL POSITION

This is where the financial plan starts to come together. It is the springboard of any financial plan. It has a significant bearing on a financial plan and the advice emanating from the plan. At the outset a review of the current financial position of a person can provide an indication of whether the objectives discussed and formulated, are realistic. The objectives may need to change when the current financial position of an individual becomes known. It also provides an insight as to the knowledge an individual has about money and can provide information on their attitude to risk, debt and savings. The current financial position has two separate parts. The first is to determine the **net worth of an individual** at the current time. This is simply the individual's value in terms of the difference between assets owned and debts owed. The second stage focuses on the individual's **personal earnings** – the earnings of the individual and their assets, relative to their expenditure on consumables, investments, pensions, savings and debt repayments. All cash flows should be included.

Personal assets

Personal assets are items that the individual owns that have value. They typically include savings, investments, properties, company share schemes and tangible assets such as jewellery, artwork, wine and motor vehicles. When determining the net worth of an individual it is common practice to list the individual's personal assets, their partner/spouse's personal assets, joint personal assets and the return being received on the personal assets in percentage terms (if known). These figures are likely to be estimates. In most instances, it would be a waste of an individual's funds to request proper valuations of assets for the purpose of financial planning only. The best approach to determining the personal assets of an individual is to provide them with a list of assets that are commonly held by individuals. The individual can then state whether, or not, they have that type of asset. The individual should be asked to place a value on the asset and to provide an estimate of the return being earned on it. Where they do not know the percentage return being earned, it might be worthwhile asking them for details of income earned and expenditure paid out on the asset yearly.

An example of a proforma asset sheet might look like the following (this list is not exhaustive):

Schedule to calculate the personal assets of an individual/couple

Assets	Individual	Partner	Joint	Current return
Land and property				
-Home			€/£500,000	
-House contents			€/£40,000	
-Other properties				
-Rental 1	€/£200,000			
-Contents	€/£5,000			
-Rental 2		€/£180,000		
-Contents		€/£1,500		
-Commercial property	€/£100,000			8%
-Agricultural land			€/£400,000	2% approx
-Cattle stock			€/£8,000	
-Forest			€/£25,000	
Other investments				
-Savings account (term)			€/£52,000	5.5%
-Deposit accounts	€/£5,000	€/£4,000		3.8%
-Credit union share accounts	€/£500	€/£2,500		4.5%
-Equity shares	€/£2,500			
-Surrender value of life policies	€/£7,000	€/£25,000		
Other assets				
-Inheritance expected		€/£200,000		
-Jewellery	€/£500	€/£5,000		
-Motor vehicles	€/£10,000	€/£6,000		
Total assets	**€/£330,500**	**€/£424,000**	**€/£1,025,000**	
Total joint assets	**€/£1,779,500**			

Personal liabilities

After listing the assets according to their category, it is recommended that similar information is obtained for personal liabilities. **Personal liabilities** are commitments made to transfer economic benefits in the future. Examples of personal liabilities include mortgages, bank loans, credit union loans, hire-purchase agreements, leasing agreements, credit card balances, store cards balances and any other. A proforma list of potential liabilities can be used to make this task easier for an individual. A liabilities schedule might include the following (this list is not exhaustive):

Schedule to calculate the net worth of an individual

Liabilities	Individual	Partner	Joint	Current cost
Secured debt				
-Home mortgage			€/£453,000	5.9%
-Rental property 1	€/£150,000			7%
-Rental property 2		€/£160,000		6.9%
-Agricultural land			€/£150,000	7.2%
-Forest			€/£10,000	6.5%
Other bank debt				
-Loan account			€/£25,000	7.5%
-Overdraft			€/£3,000	10.5%
-Credit union account			€/£3,000	6.5%
-Car loan 1	€/£8,000			8.2%
-Car loan 2		€/£5,000		7.3%
Credit card debt				
-Credit card A	€/£4,500			16.5%
-Credit card B		€/£5,200		14.5%
-Credit card gold	€/£2,000			12.5%
Total debt	**€/£164,500**	**€/£170,200**	**€/£644,000**	
Total joint liabilities	**€/£978,700**			

Therefore this individual (combined with the partner) has a total net worth of €/£800,800 made up from their total assets less their total liabilities (€/£1,779,500 − €/£978,700).

Personal earnings/cash inflows

The second stage is to consider the earnings potential of the individual, including earnings from personal assets held. Income typically comes from employment (it is the after-tax figure that is important), self-employment, government benefits, rental properties, investments, savings and any other. One-off income should also be included, such as a legacy or a gift of funds. The income will highlight cash inflows that arise from normal activities and these one-off, or exceptional items separately. An earnings schedule might look like the following:

Schedule to calculate income for an individual (and their partner) for one year

Income	Individual	Partner
-Employment – standard (net)	€/£50,000	€/£45,000
-Overtime/bonus (net)	€/£6,000	–
-Pension	–	–
-Government benefits		€/£2,400
Income from self-employment		
- Consultancy	€/£5,000	–
- Farm income	€/£5,000	€/£5,000
Income from property		
- Rental income	€/£3,000	€/£3,500
Total investment income		
- Interest on savings	€/£1,144	€/£1,144
- Deposit account	€/£152	€/£122
- Dividend on credit union account	€/£23	€/£112
- Dividends	€/£300	–
Total income	**€/£70,619**	**€/£57,278**
Total joint income	**€/£127,897**	

This individual, and their spouse, have income from a variety of sources. They are employed, undertake some consultancy work, have rental properties, farm land and have investment income. In addition, they receive some universal government benefits for having children (for example, the family allowance in the UK). Their total joint income amounts to €/£127,897.

Personal expenditure/cash outflows

It is also important to get an indication of the current outgoings of the individual (and their partner) before advice can be provided. The same principle applies – ongoing expenditure such as the grocery bill and house bills should be highlighted and one-off cash outflows, such as paying for a holiday, should be separately identified. Expenditure might include the following:

Schedule to calculate expenditure for an individual (and their partner) for one year

Expenditure	Individual	Partner
House running expenses	€/£12,000	€/£2,000
Repairs	€/£300	€/£500
Mortgage	€/£19,200	€/£19,200
Insurances	€/£2,000	€/£1,500
Rental property mortgages	€/£13,400	€/£14,500
Rental property expenses	€/£2,000	€/£2,000
Land expenses	€/£4,000	€/£4,000
Loan repayments	€/3,000	€/£3,000
Credit card	€/£2,600	€/£2,900
Credit union	€/£1,200	€/£1,200
Car loan	€/£4,800	€/£3,000
Car tax	€/£200	€/£180
Car insurance	€/£1,000	€/£800
Car fuel	€/£3,120	€/£2,200
Travel and leisure	€/£3,000	€/£1,800
Clothing and presents	€/£2,000	€/£4,000
Education	€/£1,500	€/£1,500

Schedule to calculate expenditure for an individual (and
their partner) for one year (continued)

Expenditure	Individual	Partner
Charitable donations	€/£1,000	€/£800
Private pension	€/£1,300	€/£800
Additional taxation	€/£2,000	€/£1,800
Total expected expenditure	**€/£79,620**	**€/£67,680**
Total joint expenditure	**€/£147,300**	

Note: a more detailed cash expenditure budget proforma is provided
in the appendix to this chapter.

The total joint income per year for this couple is €/£127,897 and
the total joint expenditure is €/£147,300. Therefore, this individual and his spouse have outgoings of €/£19,403 more than
their cash inflows. This situation cannot continue. In addition,
if the assets and liabilities are analysed, it is clear that they
are operating with an overdraft; hence do not have money in
their current account. This situation will only worsen as time
goes on. A key aim at this stage, regardless of the objectives
set, would be to reverse the net cash outflow situation. The
case study at the end of this chapter provides an example of
the type of advice that might be provided to an individual after
assessing their financial plan.

IDENTIFYING VARIOUS COURSES OF ACTION
AND ANALYSING THEM QUANTITATIVELY

To assist an individual in deciding on their final financial plan,
it is important to prepare a financial plan which projects the
result of the current spending, debt and savings policy into
the future, assuming the individual will continue with this

policy into the future. This is called **cash flow planning** or **cash flow projections**. The outcome of this should be interpreted in light of the individual's primary and secondary objectives. When projecting cash flows the preparer has to adjust the data to take account of inflation, future earnings increases, expense increases and life expectancy. These adjustments are subjective.

Cash flow projections and budgeted statements of net worth should then be prepared to show the expected outcome, assuming the advice given, is adopted. The plan should highlight the best ways to make use of existing resources and possibly take into account changes that the individual agrees to make which impact on their finances. This should be compared to the projected financial position calculated under the first paragraph and interpreted in light of the financial objectives set. It may be that the objectives require revising, or the financial plan is changed so that the individual achieves their objectives.

The plan might predict future cash flows and net worth under a variety of periods (one year, five years, ten years, on retirement, etc.) and for a variety of options. One option may be to analyse the impact of pursuing some secondary objectives and dropping others. Steps may be identified that can help the individual achieve their objectives. For example, the consequences of increasing/reducing mortgage repayments, the consequences of increasing/reducing the pension contributions, the consequences of reducing expenditure on non-essential items, the savings to be made by managing debt, the additional income that can be generated from suggested investments, can all be factored into the projections, either together or separately, as a series of 'what if' scenarios. In terms of major life changing events, the cost of having one, two, three, etc. children can be included, as can the impact of an individual retiring early. Some individuals may have early retirement as their objective, with a particular lifestyle in mind, so the financial requirement to allow early retirement can be highlighted.

SELECTING AND IMPLEMENTING A COURSE OF ACTION

The financial adviser should agree one course of action with the individual and prepare a final financial plan based on this agreement. The plan should include a summary of the profile of the individual, should detail their primary and secondary objectives, should highlight their current net worth, should outline the steps taken to improve their financial position, should list the assumptions made and provide a financial budget outlining the expected revenues and outflows and the expected net worth at the end of one year, possibly in five years, and may even project the expected net worth in the year the individual is expected to retire.

In general a financial plan should cover the following main themes:

- Background to the individual, including risk assessment
- Financial analysis of the individual's financial position
- Debt management
- Savings
- Investments
- Taxation
- Risk-management (insurances)
- Education planning (if dependents)
- Problems and issues (dependents/care)
- Retirement planning
- Succession planning
- Review process

The plan also needs to be written in a clear and concise manner which is understandable to the individual.

MONITORING THE SITUATION IN THE FUTURE

Discussing the impact of deviations from the financial plan at the preparation phase, when a variety of scenarios are considered, is beneficial for an individual, as it makes them more aware of the impact of deviations from the plan. Even though this stage raises an individual's financial awareness, it is good practice to arrange a review of the position at some agreed date in the future. This may coincide with the planned achievement of a secondary objective, such as purchasing a property, or may simply be after an agreed timeframe, such as in one year's time.

Individuals should be encouraged to review their own position, on a monthly or quarterly basis, to identify if actual progress is according to plan. Many steps can be automated, for example savings and pension contributions can be set up using direct debits, as can changes to debt repayments. Care is required when automating these functions as the cost of going into an overdraft is punitive. Individuals should be encouraged to keep an emergency reserve to cover unforeseen costs. An individual may have liquidity problems if they overestimate their income, or underestimate their costs when preparing the financial plan. It is important to be realistic at this stage and not to prepare a wish list.

Individuals with business acumen should be encouraged to set up their own personal budget on a spreadsheet and to update this regularly. This will ensure that their finger is on the pulse of their own financial health.

TAKING REMEDIAL ACTION

If at the review stage, it is clear that the initial financial plan is no longer valid (because the individual's situation has changed, or unforeseen circumstances have arisen, or the estimates were incorrect, or the individual did not make the suggested changes), then the plan needs to be re-prepared on the new basis and the individual should be made aware of the consequences of the changes made to their financial plan, on their ability to achieve their specified objectives.

CONCLUSION

A financial plan consolidates information about an individual (and their partner) in one document. It summarises their financial aims and aspirations and formalises how these can be financed. The process of setting the aims and analysing the resources available can confirm whether the aims are achievable. The plan also sets out the steps that need to be undertaken to achieve them. Alternatively, at this stage it may become clear that the aims and aspirations are unrealistic. The individual then needs to change their financial objectives to achievable ones. The planning process should try to highlight inefficiencies in an individual's finances and suggest ways of becoming more financially efficient. The suggestions should be flexible and agreed by the individual. The plan should consider savings, investments, debt management, pensions, insurances and succession planning (wills and trusts). Taxation is a major issue which should be factored into each scenario. The process of preparing a financial plan should make the individual more aware of the personal finances and the consequences of actions taken now on their future.

CASE STUDY

WORKED EXAMPLE   (Preparing a financial plan)

Kieran lives in his own home (worth €/£500,000). He has a €/£300,000 mortgage which he is repaying at €/£1,800 per month (€/£400 is capital). He has €/£2,500 in the bank, €/£3,000 in the local credit union, €/£15,000 in savings and a rental property valued at €/£180,000 (no debt). Kieran's net salary is €/£2,800 per month from his employment. He also gets an income of €/£400 per month from the rent of the investment property. He receives a dividend of 3.8% on his credit union share account and he receives 4% interest (net) on his deposit account balance.

Required

a) Prepare a statement of Kieran's net worth.
b) Prepare a statement of Kieran's projected cash flows for the coming year.
c) Prepare a statement of Kieran' projected net worth at the end of the year (assume that there has been no increase in the capital value of the properties in the year).
d) Identify any manipulation you would suggest in his assets and liabilities that might increase his personal net worth. Use estimates where appropriate. *(Note: a variety of outcomes are possible).*

e) Identify questions that you, as his financial adviser, would need answered before analysing the situation further.

Solution

a) *Statement of current net worth for Kieran*

Assets	*Kieran*	*Current return*
Home	€/£500,000	
Rental property	€/£180,000	
Current account	€/£2,500	
Deposit account	€/£15,000	4.0%
Credit union account	€/£3,000	3.8%
Total assets	€/£700,500	
Liabilities		
Mortgage	(€/£300,000)	
Total liabilities	(€/£300,000)	
Net worth	**€/£400,500**	

b) *Cash budget for Kieran (yearly – year one)*

Income	*Kieran*
Wages (€/£2,800 × 12)	€/£33,600
Rent (€/£400 × 12)	€/£4,800
Credit union interest (€/£3,000 × 3.8%)	€/£114
Savings (€/£15,000 × 4% net)	€/£600
Total income	*€/£39,114*

b) *Cash budget for Kieran (yearly – year one)* (continued)

Cash outflows	Kieran
Mortgage (€/£1,800 × 12)	(€/£21,600)
Tax on rental (€/£100 × 12 – estimate)	(€/£1,200)
Living expenses (€/£700 × 12)	(€/£8,400)
Travel, leisure and other (€/£300 × 12)	(€/£3,600)
Total outgoings	*(€/£34,800)*
Surplus expected in year 1	**€/£4,314**

c) *Kieran's projected net worth at the end of the period*

Assets	Kieran
Home	€/£500,000
Rental property	€/£180,000
Current account[1]	€/£6,214
Deposit account	€/£15,600
Credit union account	€/£3,000
Total assets	*€/£704,814*
Liabilities	
Mortgage	*(€/£295,200)*
Total liabilities[2]	*(€/£295,200)*
Net worth	**€/£409,614**

1. This represents the opening balance plus the surplus cash from the year (€/£2,500 + €/£4,314 − €/£600). The interest on the deposit account will most likely be credited to the deposit account.
2. The mortgage balance will have decreased by the capital portion of the monthly repayment for the year to €/£295,200 (€/£300,000 − (€/£400 x 12)).

d) *The suggested changes to Kieran's current financial position are provided in the following net worth table:*

Assets	Kieran	Change	Amended current position
Home	€/£500,000		€/£500,000
Rental property	€/£180,000		€/£180,000
Current account[1]	€/£2,500	(€/£2,000)	€/£500
Deposit account	€/£15,000	(€/£15,000)	–
Credit union account	€/£3,000	(€/£2,000)	€/£1,000
Total assets	*€/£700,500*		*€/£681,500*
Liabilities			
Mortgage – residential	(€/£300,000)	€/£109,000	(€/£191,000)
Mortgage – rental		(€/£90,000)	(€/£90,000)
Total liabilities[2]	*(€/£300,000)*		*(€/£281,000)*
Net worth	**€/£400,500**	–	**€/£400,500**

The changes are explained as follows (it is assumed that Kieran is single, is in his thirties, is adverse to risk and is in good health):

At present the mortgage is costing Kieran 5.6% per annum (estimate – the interest portion of the repayment for the year is €/£16,800 (€/£1,400 × 12). When this is divided by the amount outstanding, €/£300,000, a rate of 5.6% results (€/£16,800/€/£300,000). This interest charge is higher than the interest being received on the deposit account, the credit union account and on the current account. It is also noted that there is no debt on the rental property and the consequence of this is that Kieran has to pay tax on the full rental amount (less relevant expenses).

The first suggestion might be to rearrange the mortgage and to reallocate some of the debt as a charge on the rental property. €/£90,000 might be suggested. This could be obtained as an interest only mortgage (for now). As the capital value of the property is €/£180,000, obtaining this arrangement should not be difficult (50% secured mortgage). Assuming the interest on a mortgage on the rental property can be obtained for 6% (interest on rental properties is usually slightly higher than interest charged on loans on residential properties) then the total interest charge on the rental property would be €/£5,400 per year (€/£90,000 × 6%). This amounts to a monthly interest payment of €/£450. This will more than cover the rent being received of €/£4,800 and leaves room for growth in rent from €/£400 to €/£450 per month in future years. The excess of the interest over the rent can be carried forward as a tax loss to be offset against future profits. This cushion of losses will ensure that this mortgage does not have to be renegotiated for a considerable period into the future.

The mortgage is currently sitting at €/£300,000 but this will fall to €/£210,000 because of the re-mortgaging of the rental property. In addition, it would make economic sense for Kieran to use most of the funds he has in his current account, his credit union account and in his savings to reduce the balance further. He should be encouraged to withdraw a total of €/£19,000 from his bank accounts (€/£2,000 from his current account, €/£2,000 from the credit union account and €/£15,000 from his savings account) and to use this to reduce the amount outstanding on his residential mortgage. This would mean that his new mortgage on the residential property would be on €/£191,000 (€/£210,000 − €/£19,000)[1].

Assuming that Kieran retains the €/£400 capital repayment, this means that his overall repayment on the mortgage/mortgages would fall from €/£21,600 per year to €/£20,896.

1. ROI only − Kieran will qualify for yearly mortgage interest relief of €/£600 on his interest payments (€/£3,000 × 20%) assuming he purchased his property more than seven years ago (2008 rates). This relief will be given at source and amounts to €/£50 per month.

Rental property		
interest	€/£90,000 × 6% =	€/£5,400
Residential property		
capital	€/£400 × 12 =	€/£4,800
Residential property		
interest	€/£191,000 × 5.6% =	€/£10,696
Total repayment		€/£20,896

The total residential mortgage repayment would be €/£15,496 (€/£4,800 + €/£10,696), or €/£1,291 per month (€/£15,496/12). This results in a saving in cash flows of €/£704 per annum (€/£21,600 − €/£20,896).

In addition there will no longer be any tax due on the rental income resulting in a further cash saving of €/£1,200, but Kieran will receive less interest income from his bank accounts.

A full summary of the impact of this change on income is shown below. Kieran can at this stage decide whether he wishes to keep the capital repayments as they are (€/£400 per month) and can reap a stronger increase in his yearly cash, savings and investment accounts or could start a pension. He will have less interest income in the earlier years, but this will increase over the years again as the current cash surplus contin-ues to be invested.

Alternatively, he could elect to increase his capi-tal repayments by approximately €/£158 each month ((€/£1,200 + €/£704)/12) without his current stand-ard of living being affected. An increase in the capital repayments will reduce the length of the mortgage and leave Kieran in a stronger financial position when he is older.

Given the new restructured financial position, Kieran's cash inflows will change to (assuming the surplus cash will not be used to increase the capital repayments on the mortgage):

Income	Adjusted	Before
Wages (€/£2,800 ×12)	€/£33,600	€/£33,600
Rent (€/£400 × 12)	€/£4,800	€/£4,800
Credit union dividend (€/£1,000 × 3.8%)	€/£38	€/£114
Savings interest	–	€/£600
Total income	€/£38,438	€/£39,114
Cash outflows		
Mortgage – residential	(€/£15,496)	(€/£21,600)
Mortgage – rental	(€/£5,400)	–
Tax on rental (estimated)	–	(€/£1,200)
Living expenses (€/£700 × 12)	(€/£8,400)	(€/£8,400)
Travel, leisure and other (€/£300 × 12)	(€/£3,600)	(€/£3,600)
Total outgoings	(€/£32,896)	(€/£34,800)
Surplus expected in year 1	€/£5,542	€/£4,314

Kieran will be better of by €/£1,228 per year (€/£5,542 − €/£4,314). *Note: there may be set-up fees in the first year to renegotiate the mortgage – this is not included above.* This review did not consider Kieran's expenditure and it is likely that Kieran's salary and rental income will increase in the future; therefore, the cash savings should be utilised and a minimum balance left at this stage as these are likely to build up quite quickly over the coming months/years.

Summary of key actions

The surplus from each year should be used to increase Kieran's savings in the first instance (until a suitable emergency reserve is established), to start higher return investments and a pension. As mentioned previously, Kieran might also opt to increase the capital repayments on his residential mortgage. This will reduce his cash flow risks in the future as his debt will be lower.

e) The suggested changes outlined in d) above assume that Kieran is a young, single man in his thirties. A financial adviser would be interested to build up more background information on Kieran than is given in the question. Questions he might ask include:

- What are your contact details?
- What age are you?
- Are you married/do you have a partner who cohabits with you or are you likely to get married/likely to have a partner who will cohabit with you?
- If married/cohabiting, is the relationship solid?
- Have you any dependents (children, elderly parents)?
- If you have dependents – have you taken any steps to ensure that the future financial commitments relating to the dependents are covered (provision for education expenses, provision for elderly care home expenses)?
- What are your work prospects (elaborate)?
- What are the details of your current employer?
- What is your attitude to risk (complete a risk assessment questionnaire)?
- What are your long-term financial objectives?
- Have you any immediate financial objectives (are you thinking of purchasing a motor vehicle, property, for example)?

- How much of an emergency fund do you wish to keep liquid?
- What are your views on succession – have you considered making a will/do you have a will?
- What are your views on securing an income in the event of becoming critically ill, etc. (discuss insurance cover)?
- Confirm the extent of his assets.
- Confirm the extent of his liabilities (ask about credit cards, etc.).
- Go through a checklist of common types of income and expenditures to ensure the figures in the cash flow projections are accurate estimates. Identify any cash savings that could be made.

- Do you have an occupational pension scheme (obtain details)?
- What pension income would you like to have, what are you willing to give up now to achieve this?
- Have you considered your own care when elderly (the importance of this question will depend on the age of the individual)?
- Do you expect to receive any legacies?
- Are you taxable under UK/ROI legislation only?
- Who are your professional advisers (obtain details)?

KEY TERMS

Cash flow planning
Cash flow projections
Critical risk factors
Earnings risk
Financial commitments
Financial plan
Investment risk

Net worth of an individual
Personal assets
Personal earnings
Personal liabilities
Risk
Secondary objectives

REVIEW QUESTIONS

(*Answers to review questions are provided in Appendix three*)

1. Outline the key factors that should be considered in a financial plan.
2. What financial strategies might an individual undertake to achieve financial independence?
3. Explain risk in the context of a personal financial plan.
4. Personal financial plan
   A self-employed local businessman approaches you for advice on his personal finances. He supplies you with the following list of his investments, insurances and debt.

   Investments

Credit union share account (4%)	€/£3,000
Deposit account at bank (2.5%)	€/£35,000
ISA (5.5%) (tax-free term deposit account with a €/£3,600 deposit limit each year)	€/£15,000
Current account	€/£15,000
Personal pension (€/£500 per month)	€/£45,000
Investment property (cost)	€/£70,000
Share portfolio value	€/£18,000

   Annual insurances – yearly premiums

Life assurance	€/£800
Permanent health insurance	€/£750
Voluntary health insurance	€/£500
Mortgage protection insurance	€/£450
Loan protection insurance	€/£300

   Debt

Mortgage outstanding	€/£180,000
Loan on vehicle	€/£18,000

OTHER INFORMATION

- The small share portfolio has returned an average 10% per annum over the past five years.

- The businessman informs you that his private home has a market value of about €/£400,000 and the investment property is worth €/£150,000. The investment property has been increasing in value each year. The business-man is aware of the strong return it is making and has not rented the property as he would have to spend €/£10,000 now to make it attractive to tenants. The property could only be rented for €/£500 per month and the businessman considers that it would not be worthwhile undertaking the initial investment. The mortgage is secured on the private home.

- The general household costs are all purchased using the Visa card and amount to about €/£1,500 per month. The businessman pays €/£1,200 each month off the Visa bill. The outstanding balance has crept to €/£12,000. The Visa card company only charges 1% per month on outstand-ing balances. The businessman regards this as not bad value.

Required
Prepare an opening statement of affairs for the business-man from the information provided above.

5 Marks

APPENDIX: PROFORMA PERSONAL CASH BUDGET (YEARLY/WEEKLY)

	Now	If you died	If partner died	On retirement
Income				
Your salary				
Partner salary				
Bonuses				
Other				
Self-employed income				
Investment income				
Interest income				
Other				
Other expected				
Total income				
Expenditure				
Home				
Mortgage/rent				
Second mortgage				
Insurances				
Rates				
Repairs				
Garden				
Cleaning materials				
Total				
Utilities				
Electricity				
Oil/gas				
Wood/coal				
Water rates/cleaning septic tank				
Telephone				
Mobile				

	Now	If you died	If partner died	On retirement
Internet				
Cable/satellite				
Total				
Food and drink				
Groceries				
Drink				
Eating out				
Total				
Transport				
Car loan repayments 1				
Car loan repayments 2				
Petrol/diesel				
Insurance 1				
Insurance 2				
Car tax 1				
Car tax 2				
AA/RAC				
Repairs				
Tickets/parking				
Bus fares				
Train fares				
Taxi fares				
Allowance towards car				
Total				
Leisure				
Holidays				
Club subscriptions				
Cigarettes				
Entertainment				
Sports				
Books				

	Now	If you died	If partner died	On retirement
Videos				
Coffee				
Total				
Family expenses				
Day care				
Child support				
School tuition				
Pocket money				
Clothes				
Uniforms				
Total				
Debt repayments				
Credit card 1				
Credit card 2				
Student loan				
Personal loan				
Total				
Personal care				
Haircuts				
Prescription medications				
Toiletries/makeup				
Clothing				
Total				
Pets				
Food				
Insurance				
Vet				
Grooming				
Total				

	Now	If you died	If partner died	On retirement
Donations				
Total expenditure				
Surplus/(deficit)				

CHAPTER 4

THE FINANCIAL LIFECYCLE

LEARNING OBJECTIVES

Upon completion of this chapter, readers should be able to:

- Explain the meaning of the key terms listed at the end of the chapter;
- Describe how personal financial management changes throughout an individual's life.
- List life-changing events that cause financial plans to have to be revisited;
- Explain the primary focus of financial management for students;
- Explain the main financial issues facing young employed individuals;
- Explain the main financial issues facing individuals who have dependents;
- Explain the focus of financial management for established individuals; and
- Describe the financial issues facing retired individuals.

INTRODUCTION

No two financial plans are the same. Individuals may be at different stages in their financial lifecycle. They may have different financial hurdles and commitments to consider. They may have different objectives, incomes, expenses, expected lifestyles, different attitudes to the future and different attitudes to risk. Yet some common issues are typical to most, depending on the stage a person is at within their *financial lifecycle*. This chapter assumes that individuals have a financial lifecycle – they go through five different phases during their life and that the financial issues facing individuals change as they progress between phases. These phases lie along a continuum (which is more likely than not to be linked to age) and individuals progress along the continuum at different rates, depending on their initial net worth, their income, expenditure, circumstances, commitments and ability to manage their finances. The phases identified are the student phase (teens to the early twenties), the early employed person phase (teens to the late twenties), the individuals who have dependents phase (late twenties to late thirties), established individuals (forties to retirement) and people who are retired.

Rates of progression along the financial continuum are likely to be different for different individuals. For example, a student with a child or dependent adult will face more constraints than a student who enters the workforce with no commitments. They will be constrained in the amount of work they can undertake (which may affect promotion and income), will have additional costs, hence are unlikely to be able to increase their net worth at the same rate as a student who has no commitments. They are also likely to take longer to raise the funds required to purchase their own home. As there are different financial stages to each person's life, the primary and secondary objectives will change as a person progresses through life. Because of this, a person's financial plan should be reviewed and amended as they get older, or as their situation changes.

THE STUDENT

Everyone starts off being financially dependent on their parents, or the government. Very young people typically have no financial independence. This is usually the situation until a person reaches school leaving age, whereupon they go to college/university, or get their first job. It is at this point that financial planning should start to take place in earnest. At this stage also each individual should be made aware of the benefits of financial planning, as bad habits can start early. In most instances parents provide some education on managing money and try to get their children to start budgeting. Many parents, however, budget for their children, giving them funds on a drip feed basis. This does not encourage a student to take responsibility for their own financial destiny. Many students work in addition to receiving some funds from their parents. If a student has their own money, this allows them to have a higher standard of living and to have some financial independence from their parents. However, by working, a student may damage their future, as time spent working could be spent studying. Higher qualifications usually lead to higher earnings in later years.

Cash flows

Students are investing in their human capital. This is an important investment that has many costs. The largest cost is probably the opportunity cost of income forgone by not working in the years that they attend university. In addition, students usually have to move away from home and incur living costs for the first time in their lives. They have to purchase books, pay travel costs and purchase their own clothing and accessories (including phones, etc.). So students have plenty of cash outflows with limited cash inflows.

Most students are not independent from their parents, yet are at an age when they want to be. Their income is made up from parental 'hand-outs' (this does not have to be cash, but can take the form of parents paying tuition fees, purchasing clothes or a mobile phone, etc.), earnings from a part-time job, a student loan or a grant. Some students work during the summer period. The excess funds earned should be carefully managed so as to provide some financial independence during term time.

Financial management

The issues facing students are very different to those facing a person who enters employment. Their financial planning is very limited as they do not have net income to plan with. The focus in this instance would be on minimising costs and debt. Debt can be accumulated very quickly and easily at high rates. Credit cards can be a major pitfall for students. Students should aim not to have a credit card (debt and credit cards are discussed later) and only to accumulate 'good debt' (discussed in the next chapter). The main areas covered in a financial plan (outlined in chapter three, 'The Financial Plan') will also be considered, but prominence should be given to the aforementioned areas.

THE YOUNG EMPLOYED (TYPICALLY INDIVIDUALS IN THEIR LATE TEENS, OR EARLY TWENTIES)

The next category of person is the person who has started employment and typically covers the period from leaving school to their late twenties. These people either enter the workforce after school, or after university. This category of person is usually living in rented accommodation, or at home. The primary objective at this stage is usually 'to try to get on the property ladder'. This category of individual usually suffers from severe **capital rationing**. This means that the income they have available cannot cover the investments that they want to make.

Individuals who enter the workforce after university usually experience a large increase in their cash flow; however, by this stage in their life they usually have a considerable amount of debt and no saving. Managing debt is vital at this early stage in their financial lifecycle. In addition, most individuals of this age want to purchase a motor vehicle and a property. Many obtain credit to purchase a motor vehicle. This may end up as a 'Catch 22' situation – the additional debt increases the cash outflows each month, which means the individual cannot build up savings. No savings means no deposit, which means no house! If possible, an individual should use public transport until they build up sufficient funds to purchase a vehicle in cash. It is vital at this stage to emphasise the need to be frugal. A budget should be used to plan the repayment of debt, to start saving for a deposit and to start investing for retirement – even if the latter is only a small amount.

Pitfalls: debt

There are some key factors that both students and early stage employed people should be aware of. The first is that 'there is no such thing as a free lunch'. Many electrical retailers, furniture retailers, clothes retailers, or motor vehicle dealerships use pretty effective marketing to wrangle money from this section of the population. Advertising that emphasises the **affordability** of an item can cause individuals to take on too much debt (to become **over-geared**). This type of finance is easy to obtain and allows the buyer to get satisfaction from having a product immediately, without physically experiencing a cash outflow. The 'buy now, pay nothing until next year', 'zero financing', or 'this wide-screen TV can be yours for only €/£9 per week' is seen as attractive, but usually masks the true price of the product and the real cost of the finance on offer. In all instances, these items will have to be paid for, in full.

Credit cards are another huge pitfall for individuals who have just joined the workforce. Credit card debt is very accessible. Early employment individuals who are just learning the value of money should use them with care. Paying balances in full each month is the most efficient approach. Many young people get into the habit of paying the minimum payment each month. Credit cards are an expensive source of funds. A priority should be to clear high-interest credit cards. Getting into too much debt, strangles the ability of an individual to create personal wealth. However, that is not to say debt is always bad, it is not (discussed in chapter six, 'Debt Management'). An individual should always work out the total cost of each type of finance for each product, and in a separate calculation should calculate the total payments being paid out each month. This is also covered in depth in chapter six.

Pitfalls: consumable expenditure

Individuals in this category should be made aware of the consequences of daily spending on consumable items, as highlighted by the maxim *'If you look after the pennies, the pounds will look after themselves'.* A young person's long-term financial success is influenced by their day-to-day financial decision-making. For example, a student/young worker who purchases a coffee and a scone every morning in the local fancy café, would justify their action by saying, it's only a couple of euro/pounds (say €/£4-5 per day) – then they may purchase a bottle of water for the office, or the lecture class (€/£1 per day), without realising the financial implications of their actions. The €/£5 per day, equates to €/£25 per week (assuming they do this five days per week) or €/£1,300 per year. If this money is invested to earn a return of 5% then one year's expenditure (€/£1,300) would grow in value to about €/£9,152 by retirement age (€/£1,300 x 1.05^{40}).

Financial management

Advice to this category of individual will usually revolve around reducing expenditure, tackling debt, highlighting long-term issues such as the need to consider retirement, determining the type of lifestyle expected at retirement age, setting short-term goals, such as buying a house, purchasing a new vehicle, having children and vacations. It is very important for people who start taking charge of their own finances to prepare a statement of net worth and a personal cash flow budget to determine the sources of income, expenditures and surpluses. The cash flow budget can be utilised to identify potential cost efficiencies that could take place and this in turn will result in more surpluses which can be used for investment. The current debt and investment portfolio can be reviewed and advice given on whether an efficient balance of either is being maintained. At this stage of an individual's financial lifecycle, the retirement/pension decision is very important. Contributions to a pension scheme that are in the scheme longer will be worth more. Therefore, it is usually recommended that individuals join a scheme when they start their employment. Most employers offer a pension scheme as an employment benefit, with the employer contributing a proportion of the employee's salary each year. If this is not taken up by the employee, they lose the employer's contribution. Pensions are discussed in more depth in chapter nine, 'Pensions'.

At this stage financial advice is likely to extend beyond financial matters and to stress the importance of remaining healthy. With several years of life to go, the total financial requirement to service an individual in their 20s to 30s is greater. Maintaining good health increases the likelihood of working for longer at more efficient levels, hence building up more capital.

The need to retain important documentation and to organise this documentation in a systematic fashion should be stressed. Important documentation will include items such as a person's employment contract, their loan agreements, mortgage agreements, house deeds, warranty agreements, will, etc. It is important to get a systematic organised approach to the retention of these important documents, as part of an overall financial plan for the individual.

The other areas covered in a financial plan (outlined in chapter three, 'The Financial Plan') will also be considered, but prominence should be given to the aforementioned areas.

INDIVIDUALS WITH DEPENDENTS (TYPICALLY INDIVIDUALS IN THEIR LATE TWENTIES TO THEIR LATE THIRTIES)

Financial plans are not static; they change every time there is a change in an individual's circumstances. When an individual forms a relationship with another, such that their assets and incomes become intertwined (for example, moving in with a partner, a spouse, having children) or decide to take responsibility for the care of parents in their old age, then their long-term financial objectives change. The financial plan should not just focus on one individual but should take the assets and liabilities of the partner/spouse into account and should factor in the financial consequences of having children. The proforma documentation suggested in chapter three, 'The Financial Plan' has been prepared to allow the individual completing the schedules to include information on their partner, etc.

Joining a partnership

When entering into any relationship that involves a merger of assets and incomes, it is vital to consider the consequences of the relationship ending in the future. In NI, there are about 2,500 divorces each year. In the ROI the number is about 5,000 (www.statistics.gov.uk/STATBASE/). The number of divorces is increasing in each region. As regards financial settlement in the case of divorce, the Court can make a variety of orders, including lump-sum payments, periodic payments, property adjustment orders and pension adjustment orders. Recent high profile divorce cases (for example, Sir Paul McCartney and Heather Mills) highlight the financial problems that can arise when a relationship ends. If there is a clear imbalance in the assets of the parties in the relationship, then it might not be unreasonable to consider some form of premarital agreement.

After considering the impact of a separation and possibly forming an agreement to cover that eventuality, it is important to start planning with two people (or more where children are expected) in mind.

Financial planning with your partner: two incomes, no children

When the two parties in a relationship are employed, there are many economies of scale gained. There are two incomes, yet only one expense for many items, such as the mortgage, or house running expenses. Where the couple have no children they are referred to as *DINKs* (double income, no kids) and typically have an enviable lifestyle. It is more likely than not that this couple will have surplus income. They are likely to own their own property, as they will have been able to accumulate a deposit quite quickly and will be categorised as low risk by the bank, so they will have little problem in obtaining a mortgage. However, poor financial management could see this category of individual remain in a financial rut if their current expenditure increases to such an extent that it negates the impact of the surplus income they have at their disposal. This category of individual should not have any bad debt.

Financial management

Like all financial plans, the efficient use of resources will be recommended. Though this category can afford to spend more on consumables, this is only recommended if they are on target to achieve the goals that they set. These goals determine the amount they save for meeting short-term objectives – such as purchasing/replacing a car, the amount they invest for their longer-term goals (including retirement) and may include debt management (reducing their mortgage). The other areas covered in a financial plan (outlined in chapter three, 'The Financial Plan') will also be considered, however, prominence should be given to the aforementioned areas.

Children: the work versus life dilemma

When the additional costs associated with having children, coupled with the cost of working (for example, childcare, tax, National Insurance/PRSI, commuting, clothes) are taken into account, an individual could find themselves working for a salary that is actually lower than the minimum wage rate. In addition, on a psychological level most working parents

suffer stress and guilt because they elect to work. This combined with expensive childcare costs raises the question 'is it
worth working?' In some instances the lower earning partner
leaves work to look after the children. However, this decision should never be taken lightly. Leaving the workforce
might damage an individual's career. In most careers, the
role evolves over time, with new rules, regulations, products, contacts, etc., making it difficult to re-enter the workforce in the same role, or at the same position. Then there is
the future to think of. If an individual leaves the workforce,
they stop paying into their pension, as do their employers
and this will impact on the final pension they receive when
they retire. The non-financial issues also influence this decision. Some individuals could not stay at home, needing
adult company; whereas other individuals are happy to do
so and enjoy the role (reaping psychological rewards). Some
individuals believe that day-care is institutionalising children at too young an age; others feel that day-care provides
social and interpersonal skills that a child would not get at
home. The choice of whether to continue working, or to take
a career break and look after children is a personal choice, so
the financial plan should consider both options as an aid to
the decision on whether to work, or not.

Financial planning with your partner: two incomes, children

When a couple indicate that they wish to have children, this
should be factored into the financial plan. Children are a real
financial cost. A pro-rata increase in consumable expenditure can be expected, as a major outflow that will have to
be taken into account is childcare costs. Childcare costs are
typically €200/£140 per week per child (in some instances
this amount can be more, or less, depending on location and
type of childcare sought). Discounts of up to 20% are usually
available when there is more than one child.

Financial management

The financial plan will consider the resources available,
the surplus cash available, savings levels, debt levels,

investments made, retirement planning and will consider these in light of the individual's aspirations. This category of individual is likely to have surplus funds, though will also have more demands on these funds. With so many dependents, insurance becomes quite important. In addition, the decision has to be made as to whether to pay for the education of the children, or not. Investments need to be started where the couple decide to pay for their children's education. Normally a termed investment is recommended, which is organised to mature when the children start third level education.

The other areas covered in a financial plan (outlined in chapter three, 'The Financial Plan') are also be considered, and prominence should be given to the aforementioned areas.

Financial planning with your partner: one income, children

Where one partner does not work, then the financial plan will have to take this into consideration as one source of income will have to cater for the future needs of both individuals and any children. The relevant risk-reducing insurance policies (see chapter five, 'Insurance') will have to be updated and the pension company informed of the existence of the dependent spouse (pension companies normally provide a pension to widows). Unless the single income is very high, the financial plan will be constrained by income and the individuals concerned will have to accept a lower standard of living (though will consider this worthwhile as they may feel that they have a better quality of lifestyle), whilst still ensuring that a portion of their income is invested to provide them with an income in their pension years.

Financial management

Financial advice is likely to focus on analysing current money management, including identifying potential efficiencies/savings in costs. Non-essential expenses should be listed, ranked, and reduced in order of least needed. These expenses might include satellite television, broadband fees, telephones (where there is a landline plus mobile phones), entertaining (this will be even more costly now as babysitters will also require payment), travel costs (if situated within a town it may be possible to operate with one car). If after this the budget still does not return a surplus, it might be possible to extend the length of the mortgage to bring down the monthly repayments. Another option might be to relocate to a cheaper property, with a lower mortgage. The advice given will depend on a variety of factors, including the potential deficit in income, the skills of the person leaving the workforce, the likely ease of their re-entry to the workforce, the period of time that person is leaving the workforce and the investments already in place.

The financial plan will also have to consider debt management – in particular it should ensure that a sufficient level of emergency funds is kept available. It will be more difficult to build up savings from one salary, as this causes liquidity risk for the couple, so a larger buffer balance of cash is required. The plan should also try to encourage some savings and should highlight the appropriateness of the retirement fund provision. Education planning should also be discussed, though it may not be possible to fund this at this stage.

The single income period may only be for a short time (in many instances a parent stops work to look after the children when they are very young, returning when they go to school). This will be factored into the financial plan and, for example, building savings for retirement may be put on hold until the future. Depending on the level of the salary being earned by the working partner, it may be that the couple are entitled to government assistance. This should also be considered. All the other areas covered in a financial plan will also be considered but are not as prominent as those discussed above.

ESTABLISHED INDIVIDUALS (INDIVIDUALS IN THEIR FORTIES TO RETIREMENT AGE)

This category typically includes people in their forties who are on the property latter, who are paying into a pension scheme, who have investments and whose children (if any) are post-primary school level. The financial comfort of this category of individual depends on how they conducted their financial planning in their 20s and 30s. If they followed a tight financial plan, minimising costs, investing (primarily in their private property) and putting away for their retirement, then they are likely in a very comfortable financial position. These individuals probably have their own property, which they purchased at least ten years earlier and may even have upgraded in the ten-year period. Their property will have risen in value, yet the initial mortgage will be lower (after ten years of repayments). Moreover, the individual's salary will have increased, yet the mortgage repayments will be similar to those being paid ten years earlier.

Personal financial management

The issues facing this category of individual will include deciding on the type of investments and the level of pension required. In addition, at this stage in an individual's life, serious consideration needs to be given to the financial consequences on the family unit, of the death of one or both parents. A good will, detailing the wishes of the individual, should be advised with the individual being made aware of the impact of inheritance tax on their wishes (taxation advice is likely to influence the contents of the will). Individuals should be advised to discuss their wishes with future heirs as this can uncover issues and reduce bitter feelings in the future.

The **investment decision** will include looking at the current portfolio of investments, discussing the objective of each, considering the risk of the investments and advising on future action. At this stage most individuals will have moved to their target residence or will plan to move to a target residence in the near future; therefore financing this will be an important issue. Some investments may be encashed to reduce the level of debt, if necessary. At this stage another financial issue becomes imminent – the funding of third level education. Where the individuals have decided to fund their children's education expenses, then it is likely that they will be advised to pay into a termed investment, which will mature in time to pay for third level education costs. It is important to determine periodically if this investment is on track to cover the estimated costs, if not, corrective action is required.

So long as an individual is on target to meet their objectives, and have a pension and/or a sufficient portfolio of investments that is sufficient and on-track to cover the individual's retirement wants, then these individuals should have sufficient surplus funds to be able to enjoy a more luxurious lifestyle.

Individuals who are retired

When an individual retires their objectives will change again. The focus will no longer be on building up a pot of funds for the future. Individuals who have retired and who have taken financial advice in their earlier years, will now own their home outright and should have no debt. Though income has fallen, outgoings should also have fallen. The main source of income will be a private and/or work and public pension, combined with income from investments and cash from selling investments, if necessary.

The individual should also ensure that they are getting all the retirement benefits that they are entitled to. This can be quite complicated as there are several benefits available for retired individuals, many of which are means-tested (see chapter nine, 'Pensions').

At this stage an individual might wish to downsize their property in an attempt to reduce their costs and their household management issues. This will also release equity for their disposal. Some individuals will remain working as this is what they want to do (at retirement age, working for income should not be necessary), or the individual may travel. It is important to point out to an individual that travelling and working is more likely to be feasible in the earlier part of their retirement.

Key issues facing a retired person include the cost of care when infirm, funeral costs and how their estate should be distributed to heirs. At this stage, banks, building societies, credit unions, investment companies and pension companies should be informed of the name and details of the person to whom the cash or assets should pass to, in the event of death. Having a formalised financial plan throughout an individual's life will mean that they have their documents in an organised manner. If this is not the case then now is the time to put it right, so that heirs are aware of all the assets owned. It is useful to make heirs aware of the individual's updated wishes. This makes it less likely that heirs will contest the individual's wishes on death.

As with the other stages, a retired person should review their financial plan periodically as they may have to finance themselves for over 30 years!

CONCLUSION

When considering the focus of a financial plan, it is important to determine the stage in the financial lifecycle that a person is at. Though all the main areas covered in a financial plan are relevant, some are more important than others, depending on an individual's personal circumstances. In general:

- Students are advised to focus more on being frugal and on minimising their exposure to debt.
- Young employed people should also be frugal and should focus on debt management. In addition to this saving becomes important.
- Individuals with dependents have to extend their financial plan to take account of others. Their financial plan will depend on the resources available to them and the demands on these resources. Balancing the need to fund the future of dependents and putting away for retirement is important. It is likely that investment levels will be low. Having appropriate insurance is more important at this stage.
- Established individuals are likely to be focused on providing for their retirement. This will include eliminating debt before retirement. Succession planning also becomes more important than the other key areas of a financial plan.
- The whole process changes when an individual retires. It is no longer about saving, but about achieving a comfortable lifestyle from the investments and pension built up. Succession planning is very important at this stage.

KEY TERMS

Affordability	Financial lifecycle
Capital rationing	Investment decision
Economies of scale	Over-geared

REVIEW QUESTIONS

(Answers to review questions are provided in Appendix three)

1. Outline the key financial factors that should be focused on in a financial plan for a:
   a)   Student; and a
   b)   Retired individual.

2. Outline the key factors that should be considered in a financial plan by someone who is 30 years of age and who has just got married.

3. Percy is 48. He has just been made redundant. He worked for the company for 20 years and paid into its pension scheme. It is a large reputable company and even though Percy has been made redundant the company has several other factories and branches that are successful. Percy owns his private home and €/£70,000 is still outstanding on the mortgage.

   Required

   Detail the type of information that you would now include in Percy's financial plan.

4. Mary is 40. She has two children and does not work. Her husband has just passed away. He was earning €/£60,000 per year.

   Required

   You have never met Mary before. Provide a list of information that you will require, before you start to prepare her financial plan.

5. Discuss the advantages of using a detailed personal cash budget (as is detailed in the appendix to the previous chapter) to record an individual's personal income and

expenditure in yearly terms. In addition, outline the benefit of being frugal in the earlier years of an individual's life cycle.

6. You are a personal financial advisor. You are preparing to meet a client Mr. Mark Murphy and his son Peter. Mark is 52 years of age and Peter is 22 years of age and abut to graduate from college.

Required

Compare and contrast the likely financial goals and positions of Mark and his son.

8 Marks
(ICAI, CAP 1, Summer 2008, Q6 (a))

CHAPTER 5

INSURANCE

LEARNING OBJECTIVES

Upon completion of this chapter, readers should be able to:

- Explain the meaning of the key terms listed at the end of the chapter;
- Define income protection and explain how it works;
- Describe some insurance products that offer income protection;
- Describe the different types of common life assurance products;
- Explain how critical illness cover works;
- Describe the extent and limits of private medical insurance; and
- Describe payment protection insurance and explain the controversy surrounding this form of insurance.

INTRODUCTION

There are insurances available to cover virtually any risk an individual is exposed to, so long as the individual is willing to pay for them. It is down to personal choice. However, there are a number of products that are usually recommended. These are focused on in this chapter.

As individuals progress through their lives, their financial commitments and risks change. A young individual with no partner, or dependents could be selfish. They only have to look after themselves. Their focus would be on maintaining their income (income protection), ensuring that they were cared for in the event of a major health problem (critical illness) and ensuring that they have any acute health problems dealt with quickly (private medical insurance). An individual who is risk adverse is likely to opt for all the above products and possibly some more. Rather than opt for private medical insurance the individual may rely on the health service (this option is really only open for individuals in the UK, as most individuals in the ROI have to pay for their health care).

When an individual gets married, the situation changes again. At this stage the above insurances are relevant but an additional insurance 'life assurance' becomes important, as individuals do not wish to leave their partner with debt to cover on their own. Again it depends on the individual's circumstances. Where the individual has life assurance through their work pension which has a lump sum payment that will cover the debt, or has a wide range of capital assets that could be sold to cover the debt, then they are at less risk and may opt not to take out additional private life assurance. Income protection may not be as important now, as two salaries are coming into the house and the loss of one may not affect the couple's lifestyle. Again it is a matter of choice. It may be worthwhile looking at some of the investment insurance products that provide a lump sum on death, where the individual feels that their estate will be subject to a large inheritance tax bill.

When an individual has children they usually become quite risk adverse. One income may not cover the current lifestyle expense, income protection becomes more important, as does life assurance and critical illness.

Finally, when a person gets close to retirement age, they may find that they have to pay large premiums for health insurances and most of the income protection policies only operate for the working life of the individual. Retired people are usually less able to insure themselves against risks.

The main insurances are now considered in turn.

PROTECTING INCOME LEVELS

Income protection is where an individual takes out an insurance policy to protect their income level falling below their current level. This is likely to happen when the individual loses their job, or becomes too ill to work. *Family income benefit* is a policy which aims to replace the shortfall in annual income. It is not treated as taxable income on the recipient but as a capital gain – hence is subject to capital gains tax.

Permanent Health Insurance (PHI) guarantees a replacement income when someone is unable to work for medical reasons. The amount to be insured is typically the income requirement plus debt repayments, minus any income being received from other sources. PHIs typically pay between half and 2/3rds of an individual's salary, less state benefits. The amount varies depending on the policy taken. Women usually have to pay higher premiums than men because they have a history of making more claims. Some policies do not cover an initial period – possibly six months or more.

When an individual does not have valid insurance cover they are entitled to some income either from their employer, or the government, or both. The amount and rates of benefits available when ill are now outlined for the UK and the ROI.

UK: SICKNESS BENEFITS

When an employee is unable to work because they are sick, they are entitled to *statutory sick pay (SSP)* from day 4 to 28 weeks at the rate of £75.40 per week[1]. This is paid by the employer. The employer gets some relief, by getting a reduction in their national insurance contributions bill (there are some restrictions). Some employers will pay more, maybe even the whole salary. It depends on the contract of employment agreed with their employees. When the 28-week period is over, the employer is no longer obliged to provide any finance to the employee. At this stage the employee has to claim *incapacity benefit* from the government. This is changing to an *Employment and Support Allowance (ESA)* from October 2008.

When sick for periods of between 28 and 53 weeks, an individual is regarded as being entitled to short-term incapacity benefit. The amount claimable, ranges from £63.75 to £75.40 per week. Anyone who is still unable to work after this period of time is entitled to long-term incapacity benefit (amounting to £84.40 per week)[2].

ROI: SICKNESS BENEFITS

In the ROI employers do not have a legal obligation to pay their employees sick pay, though many opt to do so as a perk of employment. Individuals who become ill in the ROI are entitled to illness benefit, disability benefit or invalidity pension. If the illness is short-term then the relevant benefit is *illness benefit*. This is a contributions-based payment that

---

[1] 2008/09 rates.

[2] 2008/09 rates.

is open to individuals who have paid certain levels of social security and who are now unable to work. They are entitled to receive amounts of up to €197.80 per week with up to €131.30 for a qualifying adult. The benefit payable ranges from €88.90 to €197.80 per week, depending on the weekly income of the individual. For example, an individual who earns between €80 and €125 per week can claim €127.80 per week.

Disability is a long-term means-tested benefit, which tops the sick individual's weekly income to €197.50 per week. *Invalidity pensions* are for individuals who are classed as having a long-term illness. This benefit amounts to €203.30 per week.

It would seem from a brief review of the benefits in both regions that the benefits to individuals in the UK are not as favourable as those on offer in the ROI. Individuals in the UK are likely to embrace PHI more.

PROTECTION FROM FINANCIAL DISTRESS IN THE EVENT OF A SERIOUS ILLNESS

The rates of benefits available from the government for an individual who has a long-term illness are outlined in the previous section. The income available may not be deemed to be sufficient, particularly where the individual has debt that has to be paid periodically (for example a mortgage). An individual can take steps to reduce the risk of having to rely on benefits, or having to run down their savings to cover their current living expenses when a serious illness occurs, by taking out critical illness cover.

Critical illness pays out a tax-free lump sum on the diagnosis of a range of illnesses or accidents that may occur during the policy term. Typical illnesses include cancer, heart attack, coronary artery bypass surgery, major organ transplant, strokes and kidney failure. To qualify for this insurance an individual has to be over 18 to take out a policy, and under 65 to start a policy. The policy sold is usually for a minimum term of five years but will usually not cover an individual when they are over 70 years of age. The sum that can be insured typically ranges from about £25,000 to £500,000 (euro equivalents). The policy will pay out on diagnosis of one of the specified critical illnesses. If your illness is not on the list you will not be covered.

Critical illness cover can be attached to another product. Two common examples are fixed-term cover (with critical illness) and mortgage-protection insurance (with critical illness). *Fixed-term cover* combines critical illness with life insurance and will pay out on the diagnoses of a critical illness or on the death of the policy holder within the policy term, to the beneficiaries/estate. When the individual wants to pass the lump sum on death to their children, it is good practice to set the policy up in trust for the children. This will avoid inheritance tax.

Mortgage life cover (with critical illness), otherwise known as *mortgage protection insurance*, is a **decreasing protection policy**. The level of cover provided each year reduces roughly in line with the outstanding balance on a repayment-type mortgage. A lump sum is paid on the death or diagnosis of a critical illness. This lump sum is then used to pay off the mortgage.

PROVIDING FOR DEPENDENTS ON DEATH

Individuals who have a partner or dependents will be interested in ensuring that their dependents are not financially burdened when they die. In the prior paragraphs an option was introduced – critical illness cover was combined with life insurance. This provides a lump-sum to the beneficiary, if the policy holder dies during the term of the policy.

Another more commonly used product, life assurance, is taken out by individuals to pay a lump-sum on death, or at the end of a specified period. The policy can be with-profits, or non-profit. In a with-profits policy, the value of the underlying fund increases in line with the value of the underlying portfolio held by the insurance company. In a *basic life assurance policy,* an individual can pay one lump sum at the start, or can pay an annuity over a fixed period of time, or until death. The amount received may be a fixed lump sum which is guaranteed by the insurance company, or it may be linked to the performance of an index or portfolio of assets. Policies also have the option of being based on a single or joint life basis. The insurance company usually pays out when just one dies (the first one) or it can be set up to pay out on the death of both. Each policy is different.

For some life assurance policies death does not have to occur through the term of the policy – **whole-of-life policies** – pay out on the death of the policy holder. These policies are more expensive than term assurance policies as the insurance company is definitely paying out. A policy which only pays out on death within the policy term is called a **term policy**. There are two types of whole-of-life policies. One involves the policy holder paying premiums for a set term, after which the policy is treated as being paid-up. The lump sum will be paid on death afterwards. The other option involves paying contributions for the rest of the policy holder's natural life. Whole-of-life policies might be used to cover expected inheritance tax liabilities on the individual's estate.

Some policies pay out on death or on a specified date, which ever occurs first. These are known as **investment policies**. Many individuals take these policies out with the sole intention of building up a lump sum for the future. Their intention is not life cover. These policies can be cashed earlier than their maturity date, however, the insurance company will change a surrender fee, which makes this unattractive.

Pensions and life assurance

Most private and company pension schemes have an element of life cover. This is called the **personal pension term assurance**. The premiums are paid by the pension company.

If the pension is a company pension scheme, the life cover is usually linked to salary level in the year of death. If the pension is a personal pension (see chapter nine, 'Pensions' for a discussion of the different types of pension), then the lump-sum will be linked to fund value. When an individual has a pension with life cover, it is recommended that they top up the life cover to the amount they require. This may not be necessary – it depends on the circumstances of the individual and the level of the pension scheme fund.

Other life insurances/assurance products

There are several versions of life assurance, however, only two more are briefly mentioned in this text. **Convertible** *renewable term assurance* gives the insured person the right to extend the insurance period without further medical underwriting, or convert to an investment plan (this is useful for older people, as the medical examination required is usually funded by the individual, not the insurance company) and *increasing term assurance* – increases the level of cover in line with inflation or annually by a fixed amount. The annual cost of the premiums paid to an increasing term assurance policy usually increase also.

Finally, many companies may provide a company life assurance scheme for their employees. This scheme is usually administered by the employer on behalf of an insurance company. Except for time spent administering the policy, the company does not usually contribute to the scheme. Employees should shop around to determine if the life assurance is good value and decide whether they need it before electing to take it. Some companies pay life assurance for their employees as a perk. In these instances the annual premiums are treated as a benefit-in-kind and the employee is taxed on their value.

OTHER COMMONLY INSURED RISKS

Health

In the UK the National Health Service provides the full range of health care free for all residents regardless of their income. However, in many instances the waiting lists are long and individuals opt to take out private medical insurance to have their (or their family's) medical complaint dealt with quicker. In the ROI the health service is not free to all, and private medical insurance is a necessary expense.

Private medical insurance (PMI)

Each medical insurance contract is different and the medical service on offer varies from contract to contract and depends on the individual's circumstances. For example, people with pre-existing conditions are typically not covered for these conditions in the future. PMI typically pays for treatment for acute curable conditions. The treatment might be an operation or a short-term course of treatment. PMI does not cover long-term illness, or chronic illness. So PMI is likely to cover the diagnosis stage, but not treatment, where the diagnosis is long term.

Different PMI policies offer different levels and ranges of treatment. Usually the more you pay for, the more you get. In most instances the policy holder has to get authorisation from the PMI provider before getting treatment and may be restricted to a set number of medical care providers that the insurance company uses.

PMI can be provided by an employer as a perk, and as such PMI is treated as a benefit-in-kind and its value is taxable on the individual.

Payment protection insurance

Payment protection insurance (PPI) is a form of income protection which aims to cover debt repayments when an individual is unable to repay their debt. This insurance has received bad press over the past five years as several debt providers were found guilty of mis-selling this product to individuals, many of whom could not claim on the insurance because they did not meet the conditions for the insurance in the first place. In several instances policies were sold to self-employed who were exempt from being able to claim against the policy. In addition, it was not explained that the policy would not pay out for six months, or only paid six-month repayments.

Many debt providers only made debt available if this insurance was taken up, or at least that is what the consumers were led to believe. Indeed, several used to quote the monthly repayment on a loan gross (including this insurance premium) and some still do!, though cover themselves by showing the repayment without the insurance. PPI is considered to be an expensive form of protection.

CONCLUSION

Insurance is a difficult topic on which to advise. Most people have several demands on their funds and liquidity can be an issue. Even so, it is generally regarded as prudent for individuals to take out some form of income protection and critical health cover (Individuals in the ROI should have PMI).

Premiums to insurance companies for insurance/assurance products range in price and in quality. It is always advisable to shop around and to read policy documents carefully. When a policy document says premiums may rise in the future, or premiums may be reviewed, then assume it is likely that they will rise. When a death or illness cover is started it is important not to let it lapse, as it is more expensive to initiate these products as individuals get older.

Finally, insurance/assurance products differ in price, as they are tailored to take into account the risks associated with the individual being insured. Premiums are affected by age, gender, general state of health and risk factors. Risk indicators include medical history of family, being a smoker, a drinker, taking drugs and participating in extreme sports. All insurance/assurance companies will ask questions about these types of activities. The answers will impact on the price of the premiums. When an individual provides incorrect details, the insurance/assurance is invalid.

KEY TERMS

Basic life assurance policy
Convertible renewable
  term assurance
Critical illness
Decreasing protection
policy
Disability
Employment and support
  allowance (ESA)
Family income benefit policy
Fixed-term cover
Illness benefit
Incapacity benefit
Income protection
Increasing term assurance
Invalidity pensions
Investment policies
Mortgage life cover
Mortgage protection
  insurance
Payment protection
  insurance (PPI)
Permanent health
  insurance (PHI)
Personal pension term
  assurance
Private medical
  insurance (PMI)
Statutory sick pay (SSP)
Term policy
Whole-of-life policies

REVIEW QUESTIONS

(Answers to review questions are provided in Appendix three)

1. Explain the difference between insurance and assurance.
2. Explain the difference between a term policy and a whole-of-life policy.
3. What is the most important insurance for a family man with three children?

CHAPTER 6

DEBT MANAGEMENT

LEARNING OBJECTIVES

Upon completion of this chapter, readers should be able to:

- Explain the meaning of the key terms listed at the end of the chapter;
- Differentiate between good debt and bad debt;
- List five pitfalls that can lead to high debt levels;
- Prepare a debt schedule;
- Calculate the cost of debt using the time value of money;
- Measure an individual's debt exposure; and
- Calculate the quickest way to eliminate expensive debt, given an individual's financial position and current earnings.

INTRODUCTION: DEBT MANAGEMENT

Not all debt is considered bad. Credit referencing companies rank different types of debt; with some types of debt such as mortgages or student loans, being considered investing activities, which add value to individuals. Mortgages are discussed in detail in chapter eight, 'Investments'. In short, any debt which is used to acquire an appreciating asset, or which improves overall financial health, is generally regarded as *'good debt'*. Whereas any debt which is used to finance items that depreciate in value, or are consumed, is considered *'bad debt'*. This type of debt will lead to an unhealthy financial position and may cause financial distress.

Credit card debt, holiday loans and even car loans are regarded as examples of bad debt, even if the debt is affordable. In this day and age, obtaining debt is easy. A person can creep into financial difficulty without noticing the extent of the problem until it is too late.

The following table highlights common pitfalls that lead to a person ending up with too much debt.

Pitfalls that lead to high debt levels

Using credit for daily consumables: Unless the credit card bill is cleared each month, it is bad practice to use credit cards for consumable purchases such as groceries, fuel, or clothing. The temptation is always to buy more than is affordable, as credit card users are typically not as aware of the total amount being spent in a period. When using cash to purchase daily consumables, an individual is more aware of the amount available and is more likely to make decisions to remain with their budgeted monthly amount.

Using credit when cash is available: This is a bad habit. Some people want to hold onto cash and to use credit because the credit is available and psychologically they do not want to pay for the good just yet. However, if there is a reluctance to pay for a good now, it is likely that this reluctance will only increase after the good has been consumed.

Using debt to repay debt: Discussed below. Using credit cards to repay credit cards is not good practice. It is not dealing with the debt problem – just rearranging it, usually at a cost each time! In most instances a person ends up worse off than when they began.

Spending more than is earned: If a person takes home €/£1,000 each month and spends €/£1,400 then this will ruin their financial position. The monthly deficit might come from savings accumulated from a windfall gain made (inheritance or a gain on the sale of a property), or might come from debt sources, such as a credit card, or a loan.

Spending money you do not have: Taking out a loan to purchase something (such as a car) when there is insufficient income to cover the repayments will result in financial distress.

FINANCIAL DISTRESS

Financial distress is a reduction in **financial efficiency** as a result of having insufficient levels of cash. When an individual is being efficient with their resources, they are taking steps to acquire goods at a low rate. For example, by purchasing in bulk, an individual is able to obtain goods at a lower cost. If the individual does not have sufficient funds to purchase the items in bulk, then they will have to buy the goods at a higher price individually. Overall, the individual is worse off. Many individuals on low income purchase their electricity, or gas, using card meters. These cards can be purchased for amounts starting at €/£5 upwards. The electricity/gas sold through meters is more expensive than that which is purchased when an individual has a credit account with the utility company and pays their energy in one bill. This practice has received much attention from the government and pressure groups, who argue that the utility companies are causing financial distress. The result is that energy prices for this method of paying for supply have fallen. However, the utility companies still differentiate between individuals who can afford to pay, and those who have difficulty by allowing a discount for payment received by direct debit. Again not getting this discount is deemed to be an example of a financial distress cost.

When it is clear that an individual is experiencing financial distress, it is likely that the focus of a financial plan will be on **crises management**, whereupon steps will be suggested that reduce the debt burden and reduce the financial distress being experienced.

EFFICIENCY IN DEBT MANAGEMENT

Debt management forms part of most financial plans. To help make decisions in respect of debt it is good practice to prepare a **'debt schedule'**. This schedule details all the types of debt held (including loans from family members), the balance outstanding on the date the schedule is prepared for, the interest rate charged, the minimum payment agreed and the date that the payment has to be made. An example of a debt schedule might look like this:

Debt schedule

Debt schedule on: xx/xx/xxxx				
Debt source	Interest rate	Balance	Minimum repayment	Date due
Total				

The schedule should rank the debts. Bad debts usually have higher interest rates and should be paid off first. Where bad debt has the same rate of interest as good debt, it should also be targeted for additional repayments, before good debt is cleared. The **minimum repayment** is required to be disclosed, not the actual repayment as this information can be used for debt planning. The interest rates included should be comparable. They should reflect the **Annual Percentage Rate** (APR).

Calculating the APR

In some instances credit cards are advertised with monthly rates (the yearly APR is provided also, though may not be as prominently positioned). Advertising that the rate charged on a credit card is 1% per month, seems better than advertising it as 12.68% per year. The APR takes into account the fact that lenders always charge interest on the full balance that is outstanding, which includes the interest that they have already changed. So interest is charged on interest. For example, if you borrowed €/£1,000 at 1% per month, then in month one you would get charged €/£10 interest (€/£1,000 × 1%), in month two, however, you would get charged €/£10.10 interest (€/£1,010 × 1%) and so on. In yearly terms the amount of interest charged would be €/£12.68 not €/£12.00 as you might have expected. This problem is more accentuated the higher the interest rate.

The monthly rate can be converted to the yearly rate using the following formula:

$$\text{Yearly rate} = (1 + r)^n - 1$$

Where r is the interest rate being charged for the period and n is the number of periods.

WORKED EXAMPLE 1   (Monthly and yearly rates)

A credit card advertises a rate of 1.6% per month.

Required
Calculate the yearly interest rate equivalent.

Solution
The yearly rate of interest is:

$$((1 + 0.016)^{12} - 1) = 20.98\%$$

Calculating the APR when the repayments are fixed amounts

An **annuity** describes a certain pattern of cash flows, wherein a set amount of cash flow is received, or paid, over a set period of time. For example, if you borrowed €/£4,000 now (this is commonly referred to as the **present value** of the debt) and agreed to repay €/£1,000 every year for five years, then this would be described as a five-year annuity of €/£1,000. The total repayments amount to €/£5,000 and you might think that this repayment schedule is costing you 4% per year or €/£1,000 in total (€/£5,000 − €/£1,000). This is calculated as follows − the total cost divided by the amount received is 20% (€/£1,000/€/£5,000) as this is for five years. The cost is really 4% per year (20%/5). However, the cost is actually higher because the €/£4,000 is not outstanding for the whole five years. In fact, €/£1,000 is being paid off each year. So what you need to determine is the interest rate that is charged which equates five yearly €/£1,000 payments to a present value of €/£4,000.

The relationship between the loan received and the repayment amounts is expressed in the following equation.

Present value = annuity × annuity factor

Wherein, the present value is the amount being borrowed now. The annuity is the yearly amount being repaid and the **annuity factor** is a statistic which represents the present value of the interest rate that is being charged for the periods involved. This text is not concerned with teaching mathematics, so the annuity factors are provided in tables in appendix two for rates ranging from 1% to 30% for annual periods of up to 15 periods. To read the tables, select the number which represents the number of periods involved and go along the row that corresponds to this number of periods, until you come to the amount that equates to, or is close to the annuity factor value worked out from the above equation. When the periods extend beyond 15 periods, the formula provided in Appendix two can be used.

To return to the previous example:

Present value = annuity × annuity factor

€/£4,000 = €/£1,000 × annuity factor
Annuity factor = €/£4,000/€/£1,000
Annuity factor = 4 (five periods at X%)

By reading the tables this equates to 8% (the annuity factor for 5 periods at 8% is 3.993, which is just below the target amount of 4)

Therefore, when the cash flows and the amount that is being borrowed is known, the annuity tables can be used to decipher the actual APR that is being charged.

WORKED EXAMPLE 2 (Effective interest rate on finance)

Amanda's car insurance premium is now due. The new premium is €/£1,200 for the year. The company offers two payment alternatives. The first is to pay the full €/£1,200 immediately. The second allows Amanda to repay the premium monthly at the rate of €/£106.62 per month. Amanda considers this to be very competitive.

She explains that she is only paying €/£6.62 per month for the financing and this equates to 6.62%.

Required
Advise Amanda of the real annual percentage interest rate being applied to this finance deal.

Solution
The yearly rate of interest is:

€/£106.62 × annuity for 12 periods at X% = €/£1,200
Annuity for 12 periods at X% = €/£1,200/€/£106.62
Annuity for 12 periods at X% = 11.255
Using the annuity tables this equates to 1% per month.
   Which is the equivalent of 12.68% $(1 + 0.01)^{12} - 1)$ per year.

In many instances companies stress the **affordability** of the product they are selling, by focusing on the small size of the monthly/weekly repayment. The annual interest rate being charged is usually disclosed in the agreement, but is not highlighted as part of the marketing strategy.

DEBT MANAGEMENT: CRISES PLANNING

Debt restructuring

There is a variety of loan companies who strive to help individuals manage their debt, by bundling debt into one product, or by encouraging individuals to increase their good debt (mortgage) to repay their bad debt (credit cards). This is called **debt restructuring**.
   Repaying debt using debt is never the best solution, but repaying debt with cash is. If an individual increases their mortgage, they end up paying it off over a longer period, which will increase their outgoings over a longer period of time and reduce their ability to build up equity value in their home. This problem is more pronounced when house prices are stagnant or increasing very slowly and inflation is low, as

the value of an individual's equity does not rise with general price increases. However, when an individual is facing cash flow problems and is experiencing financial distress, then a short-term option may be to renegotiate debts, or to consolidate debts to improve liquidity so that the individual is left with some flexibility and less financial distress.

Care always has to be taken when obtaining debt, even good debt. It is vital to ensure that sufficient liquidity is maintained to fund an individual's lifestyle (assuming the lifestyle is affordable, realistic and is within the individual's overall aim), to accumulate an emergency reserve and to invest for retirement.

Debt management plan (DMP) (ROI and the UK)

A debt management plan is a government supported scheme in both the UK and in the ROI, in which individuals who have personal unsecured debts which are causing financial distress, can get financial advice on debt management (crises management). An adviser takes details of all the debts owed by the individual, notes the amounts to be repaid, the interest rates, the income of the individual, etc. and makes an assessment of whether the individual can repay. If they can, then the lenders are approached to agree to a more realistic repayment schedule. It is up to the lender to agree to the new repayment schedule. At this stage they will freeze the interest and charges that are being added to the debt. If the individual cannot pay, this option is not open to them and they will have to go into Individual Voluntary Arrangement (UK), or enter into a Formal Scheme of Arrangement (ROI).

Individual Voluntary Arrangement (IVA) (UK only)

IVAs are available to individuals in the UK when they cannot repay their debts and they do not want to be made bankrupt. This arrangement is regulated under the Insolvency Act 1986. It involves setting up a formal contractual repayment agreement between the individual and their lenders, usually for unsecured debts, and is organised by an insolvency practitioner.

Debt relief order (DRO) (UK only)

It is expected that DROs will become available in April 2009. DROs are a substitute for formal bankruptcy. They are available to people who have relatively low levels of debt (less than £15,000), little surplus income (less than £50 per month), few assets (less than £300) and who cannot get access to debt relief elsewhere. Individuals can obtain DROs through registered financial advisers, who can complete the application online. If approved, the Official Receiver will make the DRO without having to involve the court. An individual will not be awarded a DRO if they have an existing bankruptcy order, bankruptcy restrictions order, or IVA, or have had a DRO in the last six years.

Formal Scheme of Arrangement (FSA) (ROI only)

This arrangement is available to people in the ROI and it is otherwise known as an 'Arrangement under the Control of the Court'. It is similar to an IVA and 60% of creditors need to agree to the arrangement. Like the IVA it involves setting up a formal contractual repayment agreement between the individual and their lenders, usually for unsecured debts, and is organised by an insolvency practitioner.

When this agreement does not work there is always bankruptcy. **Bankruptcy** occurs when an individual legally declares that they are unable to pay their debts. Lenders may file a bankruptcy petition against the individual in an attempt to recoup some of the funds that are owed to them. This is the worst case scenario for the individual and indeed for the lender.

MEASURING AN INDIVIDUAL'S DEBT EXPOSURE

One method of assessing a person's **debt exposure** is to calculate their **personal debt ratio**. This ratio is also known as the **debt-to-income ratio** and is expressed as follows:

$$\frac{\text{Monthly spend on debt}}{\text{Net income}} \times 100 = \%$$

Where **'monthly spend on debt'** is either the total amount paid on debt in the month, or the amount paid on bad debt.

WORKED EXAMPLE 3 (Debt-to-income ratio)

R. Kyle takes home €/£2,500 each month from his regular employment and gets €/£500 per month in rent. He pays €/£400 per month to cover the minimum repayment on credit card A and €/£200 to cover the minimum repayment required on credit card B. His mortgage amounts to €/£1,000 per month, he pays €/£500 per month to the bank for his car loan and €/£100 per month to the credit union for his holiday loan.

Required

a) Calculate the debt-to-income ratio for R. Kyle for a typical month from the information provided above (calculate both versions – total debt ratio and the bad debt-to-income ratio).
b) Advise Mr Kyle as to the appropriateness of his current debt position.

Solution

a) Mr Kyle's debt-to-income ratio is as follows:

$$\frac{\text{Monthly spend on debt}}{\text{Net income}} \times 100 = \%$$

Where the total monthly spend on debt is €/£2,200 (€/£400 + €/£200 + €/£1,000 + €/£500 + €/£100).

Total income is €/£3,000 (€/£2,500 + €/£500).

$$\frac{€/£2,200}{€/£3,000} \times 100 = 73.3\%$$

The total monthly spend on bad debt is €/£1,200 (€/£400 + €/£200 + €/£500 + €/£100).

$$\frac{€/£1,200}{€/£3,000} \times 100 = 40\%$$

b) Mr Kyle is over-geared. He has too much debt. This is a risky situation to be in, as there is little left over after servicing debt to pay for living expenses, for making savings and for contributing to investments for his retirement. Mr Kyle's disposable income will be seriously affected by changes in interest rates.

As a priority Mr Kyle should be advised to focus his attention on reducing the extent of his bad debt. As a benchmark an individual should aim to have a total debt-to-income ratio of about 36% and Mr Kyle has a ratio of twice this. If Mr Kyle pays off all his bad debts, it will still take 33% of his disposable income to service his mortgage. Though this is acceptable, he should be advised to aim to reduce this further, if possible in the future.

Regardless of whether debt is good or bad, a lower debt-to-income ratio is considered favourable. As mentioned in the above example, a total debt-to-income ratio of 36% or lower is considered to be acceptable, with a total ratio of below 30% considered to be excellent. A ratio of over 40% is considered to be too high. When the ratio focuses on bad debt only, a ratio of over 10% indicates that an individual is over-geared.

CONCLUSION

Debt should never be taken lightly, it is usually easy to obtain, is costly, results in cash outflows and financial risk. Financial risk usually leads to liquidity problems and financial distress. It may even impact on an individual's personal welfare due to stress. If debt gets out of control, an individual may end up bankrupt. This will result in a black tick being placed on their credit record, which will impact on the individual's ability to access credit in the future.

Not all debt is regarded as bad. Debt that is used to increase an individual's worth is regarded as good debt, while debt that does not is considered to be bad debt. Even when the debt being sourced is good debt, an individual should not accept debt unless they can afford it. Good financial planning using projected cash flow budgeting and projected net worth statements should highlight the affordability of debt, or may identify when the item can be purchased in cash, if a savings option is taken. A rule of thumb is that cash flows spent on debt should not exceed 36% of an individual's disposable monthly income and about a quarter of this should be on bad debt.

KEY TERMS

Affordability
Annuity
Annual percentage rate (APR)
Bad debt
Bankruptcy
Crises management
Debt exposure
Debt management plan
  (DMP)
Debt restructuring
Debt schedule

Debt-to-income ratio
Financial distress
Financial efficiency
Good debt
Individual voluntary
  arrangement (IVA)
Minimum repayment
Monthly spend on debt
Personal debt ratio
Present value

WEBSITES THAT MAY BE OF USE

There are many sites that are geared towards giving advice on debt management. A couple have been highlighted here, though a Google search would provide you with a wealth of information.

For information on how to manage debt in the UK visit: http://www.debtfreedirect.co.uk/

For information on insolvency in the UK visit: http://www.insolvency.gov.uk/insolvency/

For information on how to manage debt in the ROI visit: http://www.debtfreeireland.com

REVIEW QUESTIONS

(Answers to review questions are provided in Appendix three)

1. Seamus has taken out a car loan which attracts an interest rate of 10% per year. The loan is for a one-year period, with the repayments being made monthly.

Required

Calculate the APR applicable for this loan.

2. What is the difference between good debt and bad debt?

3. Fernando has just received a pay increase that will result in him having €/£500 additional cash from his employment each month. Fernando has approached you to get some advice on the quickest and best way to pay off his credit card bill of €/£5,000. He informs you that he is paying interest on the card at the rate of 24.8% APR. At present he is paying the minimum repayment amount of €/£300 per month to the credit card company, but his repayment just about covers the current month's expenditure and the interest. The debt on the card has not fallen over the past number of months and this is worrying Fernando as he is considering purchasing a property and thinks that the bank manager will look poorly on his inability to clear the credit card and to raise a deposit. He currently has €/£2,000 in his current account, which he has earmarked for a deposit on a property.

Required

a) Calculate the monthly interest rate being charged by the credit card company.
b) Calculate the current monthly spend on the credit card on consumables by Fernando.
c) In light of your answer to b) advise Fernando on a repayment schedule to undertake, to repay the credit card debt. The debt should be repaid quickly, though should not leave Fernando having liquidity problems each month.

4. What are the advantages of an individual entering into an IVA (NI) or an FSA (ROI) when they are experiencing financial distress?

5. Debt Management: Martin

Martin is 30 years of age. He has approached you to help him to manage his debt. He informs you that he has just received a pay rise that equates to €/£500 per month. However, up to this point he was actually overspending his take-home wages by €/£100 per month (this €/£100 is being spent on cash consumables). Therefore, he only has €/£400 to tackle his debt problem.

Martin informs you that he has a mortgage which has 15 years left to run. This mortgage is being repaid at €/£1,200 per month, payable on the first of the month. The last statement showed an outstanding balance of €/£135,000 (the mortgage interest rate is 6.25%). Martin has a 10% car loan which he repays at the rate of €/£400 per month (on the 6th of each month). This loan has an outstanding balance of €/£6,000). He also has a 13% personal loan which is repayable at the rate of €/£200 per month (on the 4th of each month). There is an outstanding balance of €/£10,000 on this loan. He also has two credit cards. He owes €/£4,000 on the first (A) and €/£5,500 on the second (B). The minimum repayment on A is €/£70 per month and the minimum repayment on B is €/£110 per month. These payments are due on the 15th and 16th of each month. Martin pays €/£250 off each card, every month. The balances have not been decreasing as Martin is still using both cards. The interest rate on credit card A is 1.4% per month and is 1.75% per month on credit card B. Credit card A has a credit limit of €/£5,000 and credit card B is at its limit.

Martin has historically paid his car insurance monthly. Last month the final payment on last year's premium was paid. Martin is considering paying his car insurance over 12 months again. The yearly premium is €/£1,000. If he elects to take the finance option he would have to pay €/£94.56 per month for the year. The payment date is the 10th of each month. Martin has €/£2,000 in his current account earning 1% per year and €/£1,000 in a savings account earning 5% per year.

Required

a) Prepare a 'debt schedule' for Martin based on the information provided.

6 Marks

b) Classify the different types of debt into 'good debt' and 'bad debt'.

2 Marks

c) Advise Martin as to the most appropriate steps to take to tackle his debt problem and to become financially healthy. Show calculations to back up your advice.

(He informs you that, bar the €/£100 that he spends in cash, all his other consumable expenditures are paid for using the credit cards.)

32 Marks

Total 40 Marks

CHAPTER 7

SAVINGS

LEARNING OBJECTIVES

Upon completion of this chapter, readers should be able to:

- Explain the meaning of the key terms listed at the end of the chapter;
- Outline some practical steps that can be taken to establish a good savings policy;
- List five pitfalls that can lead to high debt levels;
- Explain the difference between a current account and a deposit account;
- Describe a number of savings products that are available that have tax breaks; and
- Describe how tax breaks are obtained.

INTRODUCTION: SAVINGS – THE PRINCIPLES

Debt management, savings management and investment management are the three key elements underlying an individual's financial success. If an individual has savings, they do not need to get into debt to obtain perishable goods. They can invest from their savings pot and they have emergency funds at hand to cover unforeseen financial requirements. Therefore, the management of savings is very important. It is good practice to get into the habit of saving from an early age. Many individuals do not save, they tend to purchase items using debt and to treat this as a form of saving. However, this ends up being very costly to the individual. Without saving it is impossible to achieve financial security. This chapter starts by outlining some practical tips for saving before providing a description of the most commonly used savings products by individuals. Particular attention is afforded to savings products that have tax breaks.

PRACTICAL TIPS FOR SAVING

- It is always good to set a *savings goal*. This provides more motivation for the act of saving. This might include accumulating sufficient funds to have a deposit for purchasing a house (the larger the deposit, the cheaper the finance), or paying a lump sum off the mortgage the next time the mortgage comes up for renegotiation, accumulating sufficient funds to pay for a family holiday (avoiding interest costs), or to pay for a car (avoiding interest costs).

- It is important to establish a separate savings account and to budget to transfer a certain minimum amount of cash to this account each month. If this is treated as a necessary cost, then it will be easier to achieve each month. If the transfer is automated then this makes it harder to skip or reverse in a month when the individual wishes to spend more.

- Saving should never involve an individual going into debt in order to save, it should involve budgeting and cutting back on unnecessary expenditure in order to meet savings targets.

- It is good practice to decide on a fixed percentage of your earnings to save and to try to stick to this each month. A benchmark of 10% is suggested, though this should be regarded as a minimum and would increase in line with an individual's future financial aims. Indeed, people who are approaching retirement age tend to save between 20 and 30% of their disposable income each year.

- When it is known that expenditure will rise in a month (for example in December), then additional amounts should be reserved within the current account to deal with this – it should not be a case of reducing savings.

- When one-off income is received, this should not be used to 'treat' the individual (as can happen!), but should be immediately put into savings as this can speed up the aim of the savings resulting in increased financial wealth and stability. This is particularly the case if the savings are going to be used to purchase an appreciating asset.

- Where an individual has to utilise their savings to cover an unexpected expenditure, this reduction in savings should be treated as a loan in the mind of the individual that must be repaid to the savings account in the future.

EMERGENCY FUNDS

A minimum level of savings should be set aside to cover emergencies. This is holding cash for *precautionary motives*. The greatest financial impact on an individual is likely to be the loss of their income, due to becoming unemployed unexpectedly. Though income will have fallen dramatically, most individuals have a fixed level of costs, the largest of which is probably their mortgage. Insurance can be obtained to cover mortgage repayments in the event of unemployment; however, this will only cover a set number of months and it takes time to get the claim sorted. It is advised that individuals accumulate a minimum level of savings that are equal to between three and six times their monthly costs. Therefore, when an individual's monthly costs are estimated at €/£2,000 per month, they should keep a minimum level of savings of between €/£6,000 and €/£12,000. Other large unexpected costs can include house or car repairs.

As well as covering emergencies, individuals should save for their retirement. The governments in both the ROI and the UK have established tax efficient saving schemes to encourage individuals to save for retirement. These schemes earn a strong rate of interest and are not subject to income tax, making them attractive (discussed later).

SAVINGS TYPES

Like businesses, individuals need to hold cash for transaction motives, precautionary motives and speculative motives. Cash for transaction motives is usually held within a current account. **Current accounts** typically offer a very low return (below inflation) and an individual's wealth will be damaged if they retain excess funds in a current account. Current accounts are working accounts that deal with the majority of an individual's transactions. As such, they typically have cheque books attached, debit cards and are used to pay bills and to receive income electronically. Individuals have to keep sufficient funds in their current accounts to deal with these daily transactions (**transactions motive**).

Cash required for **precautionary motives** (to cover cash emergencies as discussed earlier in the chapter) and to allow **speculative investments opportunities** to be taken when they arise should be held in a high-interest bearing but flexible deposit account (**instant access**). In addition, cash can be invested in savings products as part of an individual's investment portfolio. Various types of savings products are now explained in brief.

Deposit Accounts

The most commonly used taxable savings product is a *'deposit account'*. In the past these accounts were less flexible, with individuals having to leave monies untouched to receive bonus rates. Now with the advent of internet banking, competition has turned these into quite flexible products, many of which are instant access. Large supermarket and internet banking companies usually offer high rates of interest. This has caused high street banks and building societies to become more competitive and to offer rates that are not too far below the banks' lending base rate. It is worthwhile shopping around before a deposit account is selected.

SAVINGS WITH TAX BREAKS

When an individual decides that savings should form part of their overall investment portfolio, it is advisable to consider products that have been earmarked by the government for tax breaks and products that involve locking the funds away for long periods of time. The products that are/or have been earmarked for some form of government tax break in the ROI and in NI are now considered.

SAVINGS WITH TAX BREAKS IN THE ROI

The most publicised government targeted saving programme available in the ROI was the *Special Saving Incentive Account* (SSIA), an interest bearing five-year account that was available for investment by the public between the period from the 1 May 2001 to 30 April 2002. These accounts matured between 31 May 2006 and 30 April 2007. Under this scheme the government provided €1 euro for every €4 euro saved by an individual up to a deposit limit of €254 per month. On maturity the interest earned by the account was subject to tax at the rate of 23% (this was deducted by the administrating financial institution and sent to the Revenue Commissioners). The contribution to the account by the government over the life of the account was not taxed (so long as the funds were held intact for the full five years).

In normal deposit savings accounts, banks in the ROI take 20% of the gross interest payable to customers from the interest payment and pay this over to the Revenue Commissioners. This is called the **Deposit Interest Retention Tax (DIRT)**.

Certain post office (An Post) savings accounts are DIRT free, as are the dividends receivable on shares held in credit unions (up to a limit of €635) so long as the shares are in a share account that has a five-year term. Dividends received over €635 are subject to tax at the individual's marginal rate of taxation and interest received on deposit accounts held in credit unions is subject to DIRT.

Individuals who are over 65 years of age, or who are incapacitated, are exempt from having to pay DIRT on any savings product. To gain an exemption from DIRT, individuals have to complete form 54D 'Claim for Repayment of Deposit Interest Retention Tax for the year 2007', which can be obtained from any local tax office.

SAVINGS WITH TAX BREAKS IN THE UK

The tax break available is usually that interest on the savings balance is paid without the deduction of tax (**paid gross**).

Most savings products are subject to a 20% tax deduction at source. This is taken off the gross amount of interest – the investor being credited with the **net** amount (after-tax amount). Higher rate tax payers will have to pay an additional 20% on the gross interest in their tax returns. In many instances non-tax payers can complete a form (R85 'Getting your interest without tax taken off') which is sent by the bank to Revenue and Customs and allows the bank to pay the interest gross. Alternatively, the individual can claim the tax paid back using their self-assessment form, or form (R40 'Tax repayment form').

When making the decision to invest in a savings product, the gross interest rate of the product with the tax break should be compared to the net rate available on other products. For example, it is not worthwhile going for a tax-free product that provides an interest return of 2.5%, if a taxed alternative offers 5%; as the real return on the taxed alternative is higher at 3% (5% (1 − 40%)) − assuming the individual is a 40% tax payer.

Dividends received on credit union share accounts are tax free. The maximum shares that can be held by an individual is £3,000 and the maximum dividend payable is 8%.

NATIONAL SAVINGS AND INVESTMENTS DEPARTMENT (UK) – PRODUCTS WITH TAX BREAKS

Most tax-free products are issued by the *National Savings and Investments* department – a government department which offers savings and investment schemes to the general public, some of which are tax free. It is simply the government loaning funds from the public and paying a return for being able to do this. The investments are secure as they are guaranteed by the UK Government. The tax exempt products available from the National Savings and Investments Department are summarised briefly as follows:

1. *Individual Savings Accounts (ISAs):* These are offered by the National Savings and Investments Department and most financial institutions. ISAs replaced TESSAs in April 1999. Two types of ISA are available: a *mini-ISA* (which can be made up of two accounts: a cash account with a yearly investment limit of £3,000 and a stocks and shares ISA with a yearly investment limit of £4,000[1]) and a *maxi-ISA* (one investment made up of any mix of cash, stocks and shares with a yearly investment limit of £7,000[2]). In both instances the interest on the cash portion is tax-free to the individual. Up to April 2004 the investment manager managing the stocks and shares ISA could claim back a 10% tax credit on dividends paid into the ISA from the underlying investments; however, this tax break is no longer available. The yearly investment limit for cash ISAs for the tax year 2007/08 was increased in the March 2008 budget to £3,600, with the overall limit for the combined total of the cash ISA and the equity ISA set at £7,200. This means that the tax-free amount that can be invested in equity ISAs has actually fallen in 2008 to £3,600, assuming individuals will opt to maximise the investment in their cash ISA.

2. *Index linked savings certificates:* These are inflation beating saving certificates with tax-free returns that are issued by the National Savings and Investments Department. At the time of writing these products offered an interest rate of 1.35% above the Retail Price Index (RPI). An investor can invest between £100 and £15,000 in these products for terms of between three and five years. They are free from

1. 2007 rates
2. 2007 rates

income tax and capital gains tax (so long as the investor holds the product for a period of more than one year).

3. *Fixed interest savings certificates:* These allow individuals to invest lump sums, at pre-determined guaranteed rates of interest that are set by the National Savings and Investments Department. An investor can invest between £100 and £15,000 in these products for terms of two to five years. They are free from income tax and capital gains tax. At the time of writing the National Savings and Investment Department were offering interest rates of circa 3.2%.

4. *Premium bonds:* These are £1 bonds that are issued and administered by the National Savings and Investments Department. The public can hold between £100 and £30,000 in premium bonds. Premium bonds do not offer interest or capital growth. The bonds are entered into a prize draw which takes place twice in each month. At the time of writing each draw has a one million pound main prize and over 500,000 other smaller prizes, which start at £50. The prize winnings are tax-free. It is highlighted that the capital portion of this investment will decrease over time and winnings are not guaranteed.

5. *Children's bonus bonds:* Parents can invest between £25 and £3,000 in children's bonus bonds for terms of five years which end on the child's 21st birthday. The interest rate is fixed for each five-year period at the outset and a bonus is payable at the end. At the time of writing the National Savings and Investment Department was offering an annual equivalent rate of circa 4.05%. The return is tax-free to both parent and child so long as the investment is held for five years, or until the child is 21. No interest is payable if the bond is liquidated within the first year.

OTHER TAXABLE PRODUCTS ON OFFER FROM THE NATIONAL SAVINGS AND INVESTMENTS DEPARTMENT (UK)

1. *Fixed rate savings bonds* have a guaranteed return for amounts invested over either one, three or five years. The interest is taxable and is paid net of tax. At the time

of writing the tiered returns ranged from 4% to 4.55% (AER) depending on the term. Longer-term investments (over five years) offer lower guaranteed rates. Individuals can invest between £500 and £1 million in these bonds.

2. *Income bonds:* An income bond provides a monthly income to the investor. An initial capital lump sum of between £500 and £1 million can be invested to provide a monthly income over a term (no set term). The interest rates awarded by the National Savings and Investment Department are tiered, depending on the size of the savings. At the time of writing interest rates ranged from 5.06% to 5.33% (AER). Interest is taxable and is paid gross.

3. *Capital bonds:* A capital bond provides a guaranteed return on a lump-sum investment that is invested for a fixed term of five years. At the time of writing, this product provided an interest rate return of 4.2% (AER). The interest is taxable and is paid gross (the taxpayer has to pay the tax at the end of the tax year through their self-assessment return).

4. *Pensioners guaranteed income bonds:* Individuals who are over 60 years of age can invest between £500 and £1 million in pensioners guaranteed income bonds. They invest a lump sum and receive a guaranteed monthly income over a set term which can range from one to five years. The interest on this product is taxable and is paid gross. At the time of writing interest rates allowed by the National Savings and Investment Department ranged from 4.23% to 4.44% (AER).

5. *Investment account:* The National Savings and Investment Department also offer an 'Investment Account' (passbook account that can be accessed through the post office, by post or by standing order). Between £20 and £100,000 can be invested. There is no set term. Interest rates are variable and at the time of writing ranged from 3.7% to 4.6%. The interest is taxable and is paid gross.

6. *Easy access savings account:* The National Savings and Investment Department also offer an instant access deposit account called the 'Easy Access Savings Account'. Individuals can invest between £100 and £2

million (£4 million for a joint account). There is no set term. The interest is taxable, is paid gross and the rates are variable. At the time of writing the rates ranged from 2.35% to 4.9%.

CONCLUSION

Good financial management involves being able to save funds on a regular basis. Just as liquidity is important for companies, it is equally important for individuals. All individuals should hold at a minimum a safety level of easily obtainable funds, called an emergency fund. This ensures that individuals do not leave themselves vulnerable to financial distress. Though an individual may have a number of investments, they will still damage their wealth if they do not ensure that they retain liquidity at the correct level. Investments that are cashed early usually incur penalties. Having a sufficient level of funds in savings ensures that this does not happen.

Savings should be managed to maximise the return being earned on them (interest). This means holding appropriate levels of cash in a current account, an instant access deposit account and in a fixed-term deposit account. Good financial planning with the use of cash flow budgets should allow an individual to manage this efficiently. The use of internet banking has made cash and savings management quick, flexible and easy.

KEY TERMS

Capital bonds
Children's bonus bonds
Current account
Deposit account
Deposit Interest
   Retentions Tax (DIRT)
Easy access savings
   account
Emergency funds
Fixed interest savings
   certificates

Fixed rate savings bonds
Income bonds
Index linked savings
   certificates
Individual Saving
   Account (ISA)
Instant access savings
   account
Investment account
Maxi-ISA
Mini-ISA

National Savings and
Investments Department
Pensioners guaranteed
income bond
Precautionary motives
Premium bonds

Savings goal
Special Savings Inventive
Account (SSIA)
Speculative motive
Transactions motive

WEBSITES THAT MAY BE OF USE

For information on investment products on offer at PostBank
(a bank which deals with An post accounts and Fortis investment products) visit:
http://www.postbank.ie/

For information on products on offer from the National
Savings and Investment Department visit (rates change
regularly):
http://www.nsandi.com/

If you Google any bank you will be able to see a wide range
of savings products.

REVIEW QUESTIONS

(Answers to review questions are provided in Appendix three)

1. It is considered that individuals might hold cash for transactions motives, precautionary motives or speculative
   motives.

   Required

   Explain what this means and provide an example of each
   motive.
2. Outline the difference between a current account and a
   deposit account.
3. List the savings products available in your jurisdiction
   that have tax breaks (UK/ROI)?
4. Personal financial plan (this question covers all the information covered to this point in the text)
   A self-employed local businessman approaches you
   for advice on his personal finances. He supplies you

with the following list of his investments, insurances and debt.

Investments

Credit union share account (4%)	€/£3,000
Deposit account at bank (2.5%)	€/£35,000
ISA (5.5%) (tax-free term deposit account with a €/£3,600 deposit limit each year)	€/£15,000
Current account	€/£15,000
Personal pension (€/£500 per month)	€/£45,000
Investment property (cost)	€/£70,000
Share portfolio value	€/£18,000

Annual insurances – yearly premiums

Life assurance	€/£800
Permanent health insurance	€/£750
Voluntary health insurance	€/£500
Mortgage protection insurance	€/£450
Loan protection insurance	€/£300

Debt

Mortgage outstanding	€/£180,000
Loan on vehicle	€/£18,000

OTHER INFORMATION

- The small share portfolio has returned on average 10% per annum over the past five years.

- The businessman informs you that his private home has a market value of about €/£400,000 and the investment property is worth €/£150,000. The investment property has been increasing in value each year. The businessman is aware of the strong return it is making and has not rented the property as he would have to spend €/£10,000 now to make it attractive to tenants. The property could only be rented for €/£500 per month and the businessman considers that it would not be worthwhile undertaking the initial investment. The mortgage is secured on the private home.

- The businessman has just signed a loan agreement to purchase a vehicle (the agreement gives a 14-day withdrawal period). The loan on the vehicle is repayable at the rate of

€/£1,400 per month for 15 months. The payments do not include loan protection insurance, which is being paid for separately at the rate of £30 per month. The businessman was able to purchase the car for €/£18,000, so long as he took the finance deal, otherwise the car would have cost €/£19,000. He reckons he got a great deal!

- The life assurance is being paid over the year at the rate of €/£80 per month.

- The permanent life insurance is being paid at the rate of €/£70 per month.

- The voluntary health insurance is being paid at the rate of €/£43.75 per month.

- The mortgage protection insurance is being paid at the rate of €/£37.50 per month.

- The mortgage repayment is €/£900 per month. This is an interest only mortgage. The businessman has been paying it for the past five years.

- The businessman informs you that his take-home salary from his business is €/£3,500.

- The general household costs are all purchased using the Visa card and amount to about €/£1,500 per month. The businessman pays €/£1,200 each month off the Visa bill. The outstanding balance has crept to €/£12,000. The Visa card company only charges 1% per month on outstanding balances. The businessman regards this as not bad value.

- Inflation is currently at 2% per year.

Required

a) Prepare an opening statement of affairs for the businessman from the information provided above.

5 Marks

b) Prepare a schedule of debt to be utilised by the businessman during the year showing the cost of each source.

12 Marks

c) Prepare a personal cash budget for the businessman for the coming year based on the above information.

8 Marks

Total 25 **Marks**

5. Personal financial plan (this covers all the information covered to this point in the text)

Using the information provided in question four:

a) Provide advice on how the businessman could better manage his finances and his investments. Highlight other information you would be interested in finding out about the businessman and specify how this might influence your advice.

25 Marks

b) Prepare a statement to show the new expected statement of affairs at the start of the year assuming the advice given in part a) is acted on immediately. In addition, prepare a revised typical yearly personal cash flow budget for the businessman assuming your advice is acted on.

15 Marks

Total 40 **Marks**

CHAPTER 8

INVESTMENTS

LEARNING OBJECTIVES

Upon completion of this chapter, readers should be able to:

- Explain the meaning of the key terms listed at the end of the chapter;
- Explain the relationship between investment risk and return;
- Discuss the impact of inflation, debt, portfolio theory and liquidity on personal investment decision-making;
- Describe the ways in which an individual can invest in equity;
- Explain the differences between gilts and bonds;
- List factors that should be considered when investing in property;
- List at least four mortgage products;
- Explain how a repayment mortgage works;
- Explain how an endowment mortgage works;
- Calculate the monthly installment on a repayment and an endowment mortgage;
- Describe collective funds; and
- Explain the difference between unit trusts, investment trusts and life insurance investment bonds.

INTRODUCTION

As part of every financial plan, the **investment decision** should be considered. The relevance of this section to an individual depends on the extent of funds available after running costs and servicing debt are deducted from the individual's income. The more funds that are available; the greater the flexibility when it comes to the investment decision – hence the greater the potential to generate more wealth. Factors that influence an individual's choice of investment need to be considered before the main types of personal investments are outlined.

RISK AND PERSONAL INVESTMENT

Putting all an individual's excess cash into savings only is considered to be an inefficient investment strategy, though not risky. Risk and return are related. **Return** encapsulates income received on capital invested, a rise in the value of capital invested, or both. In simple terms, **risk** is the likelihood that the actual returns received, will differ from the expected returns on an investment. It is measured as the standard deviation of actual returns from expected returns (average returns). A larger standard deviation indicates that there is greater risk and vice versa. To compensate for uncertainty in returns, higher risk investments usually have higher expected returns relative to investments which have no/little risk. In addition, there is a chance that a risky investment will provide a higher return relative to the higher expected average return; conversely a high-risk investment also runs the risk of providing a low, or even a negative return. In most high-risk investments the capital element of the investment can fall as well as rise. It is important to gauge an individual's attitude to risk and return before deciding on an appropriate investment portfolio.

Assessing an Individual's Attitude to Risk

Questions to ask might include:

1. The current real return on your risk-free savings is, for example 2% (net rate after tax less the weighted average inflation rate for the period), are you happy with this return, or do you wish to invest in products that provide a higher return?
   (Note: the majority of investments that offer a return in excess of the risk-free rate are subject to risk)
2. Are you willing to risk a fall in the capital value of your investment? Most investments with higher returns are available when the cash invested is prone to capital increases and decreases.
3. Many high-risk high-return investments require a long-term commitment to fully gain benefit from the investment. How long are you willing to commit funds for?
4. Have you a specific funds requirement in the future that you wish to coincide the maturity of this investment with? What is the specific sum required?

5. Given your future financial requirement target, what are you willing to invest now to achieve this? *(This information can be used to determine the growth and return required, to achieve the planned financial target, helping to determine the type of investment product to suggest).*
6. Are you happy to lock away funds that cannot be accessed, unless at a cost?
7. If there are no specific financial targets, what growth/return do you wish to achieve (ideally and realistically) from the investment in more risky investments?

When evaluating an individual's risk profile it is good practice to get the individual to specify the risk they are willing to accept for each of their objectives. To this end, a scale of risks could be prepared and individuals should be asked to specify their willingness to invest in different types of products that have different risk characteristics. They should identify their liquidity requirement and highlight the proportion of their capital that they are willing to invest in a particular product. For example, a simple deposit account or government bond would be classed as having **no risk**. Within this category the products will have different levels of liquidity and the specific products to be suggested will be influenced by the individual's liquidity preferences.

Low risk usually means there will be no loss of capital, but there may be some inflationary risk to the real value of the capital that is invested. This is likely to occur where the income is pegged to the performance of, for example, the stock market, but the capital is protected. The premium is usually capped at a set level for the total period. The concern here is that, were the stock market index not to meet the predefined target, then the individual might only be entitled to the capital and possibly a smaller return than anticipated. If this return ended up at a rate below inflation, then the individual's wealth has been damaged in real terms. Fixed-return investments are the same. An investment that guarantees a return of 5% per year is only increasing an individual's wealth, if inflation remains below the individual's net return (after tax return). The net return might be 3% (5%(1 − 40%))

where the individual is a 40% tax payer. If inflation is 4%, the individual has made a loss on this investment in real terms.

Modest risk is where there is a small risk that the capital value will be eroded by a capital loss in the value of the investments. This type of investment would typically include an equity investment in blue chip securities, or unit trusts or an investment in corporate bonds. In general these types of investment incur a short-term loss in capital value which is generally reversed in the longer term.

Relatively high risk is where there is a higher level of risk that the investment might suffer a capital loss; conversely there is a higher chance that the investment will reap higher returns, relative to an investment in lower risk products. These investments typically include owning a carefully selected portfolio of shares that is deemed to be reflective of the market. Again, this type of investment requires a more long-term view if high returns are to be expected, so should not be considered if the investment is to be liquidated in the short-term. The return on this type of investment is usually linked to the success of the economy.

High risk refers to investments that have a high chance of their being a loss in the capital invested. However, these investments, if managed well and if the investor is skilled, and lucky, can reap the highest rewards. This may involve investing in certain types of companies securities, such as new starts, high technology companies, or may include investing in hedge funds, or junk bonds. Individuals who are financially secure, who have their future funding requirements well covered and who have excess funds are more likely to 'gamble' with a portion of them.

INFLATION AND PERSONAL INVESTMENT

As mentioned in the last section, an investment's net returns should exceed inflation. If this is not the case then the investment is actually eroding an individual's wealth. Hick's income theory is relevant here. If the purchasing power of capital at the end of a particular period is less than the purchasing power of capital at the start of that period, even though the absolute amount is more, then an investor's wealth is damaged. Hick's income theory regards income as the difference between the opening capital position in real terms and the closing capital position in real terms plus any capital, or income that has been consumed from the investment in the period being considered.

Depending on the inflation rate, risk-free investments such as monies invested in a deposit account, or in government bonds sometimes damage wealth in real terms. Historically, long-term investments in the equity markets provide real gains in capital wealth, though these investments are regarded as the most risky. This historical pattern of higher returns is why pension and insurance companies commit substantial funds to this type of investment.

DEBT AND PERSONAL INVESTMENT

In some instances, it is impossible to get access to a particular type of investment unless debt is used to source some of the funds. This might occur where the investment requires a minimum amount of funds. The best example is an investment in property. The general rule is that so long as inflation is positive and property price increases exceed inflation and the cost of financing the purchase of the property, then using debt to obtain the investment is recommended (so long as the yearly servicing of the debt does not lead to liquidity problems).

LIQUIDITY AND PERSONAL INVESTMENT

If an investment provides yearly cash distributions that cover the servicing of the related debt and the costs of running the investment then the investment is *self-liquidating*. This is an attractive investment, and is even more attractive if the investment is also rising in value each year. Where an investment requires a yearly cash contribution from an individual, then regardless of how attractive the future returns are, the investment should not be taken, if it leaves the individual with insufficient cash to cover their normal running expenses. Liquidity problems can cause an individual to become bankrupt, which will result in the investment having to be encashed before its maturity date, probably at a loss to the individual. There is also the personal aspect to consider, becoming bankrupt is sure to cause stress to an individual, which may result in health problems.

PORTFOLIO THEORY AND PERSONAL INVESTMENT

An individual should aim to hold a **diversified portfolio of investments**. The adage *'it is not wise to put all your eggs in one basket'* is very relevant to the investment decision process. If an individual keeps all their investment funds in interest bearing investments then the value of their income and possibly their capital will fall when interest rates decline. Likewise if an individual keeps all their investment funds in equity shares, then the value of their income and their capital will fall, when the stock market takes a down-turn. When an individual's investment pot is of sufficient size the individual should be encouraged to invest a proportion in property, in equity shares, in bonds and in interest bearing accounts. When the performance of shares, bonds and interest bearing accounts start to decline, the capital gains on property usually start to increase and vice versa. These types of investments are **negatively correlated** with each other, in other words an inverse relationship exists between their returns. Even within equities the risk of an individual's equity returns being different to market average returns can be minimised by selecting equities that have returns that are negatively correlated to each other, for example, selecting shares in an ice-cream company and an umbrella company.

To conclude, a portfolio that contains a variety of investments is more likely to provide a steady, less risky return for an individual.

THE INVESTMENT DECISION PROCESS SUMMARISED

The fundamental principles underlying investment choice need to be applied to each and every investment decision. At the outset it is important to specify the aim or purpose of the investment and the term of the investment (including an estimate of the future financial requirement from the investment). The amount that can be invested by the individual, both initially and periodically should be determined. An evaluation of these facts will help to determine the return that the investment needs to make to achieve the financial aim. At this point the feasibility of the aim will be discussed and the risk of the type of investment required to achieve the return explained. If this risk exceeds the risk identified in the initial assessment of the individual, this should be pointed out and an alternative plan prepared showing the expected investment return from an investment in the type of product more suited to the individual's risk profile. The additional contributions required to achieve the aim should also be highlighted. As with all investments, the tax implications of the investments being suggested should be highlighted.

INVESTMENT TYPES

Equities

How to buy and sell equities

Equity investments are usually bought or sold by a stockbroker, or an investment manager on behalf of an individual. A stockbroker provides an **execution only service** (the broker buys and sells without communicating with the investor) this is usually the cheapest way to obtain an equity investment. When an investment manager takes responsibility for an equity investment fund the level of individual involvement in the investment decision process varies, depending on amount of control an individual wishes to retain over the investment. The arrangement with an investment manager can be **discretionary** (wherein the investment manager ultimately makes the decisions) or **advisory** (wherein the investment manager provides advice on investment types but the decision-making is shared) or **self-select** (wherein the individual specifies the equities to invest in and conducts the trade, which can be done online, without getting clearance from the investment manager. Advances in telecommunications (broadband and the internet) allow an individual to invest in shares from the comfort of their own home using the trading platform of the investment manager's firm. Most of these trading platforms are very sophisticated, providing real-time information on share prices and share price changes. They usually highlight the movers, chart the price movement of shares, provide minute-by-minute coverage of relevant news stories on companies and allow the user to set price targets, automatic sales prices or purchase prices.

One leading UK banking institution provides an online buying and selling service for £6.95 per transaction (as long as eleven trades are conducted within a month, if not, this can increase to £12 per trade).

How to find out equity prices

The Financial Times (UK) and The Irish Times (Ireland) provide up-to-date information on equity share performance in the London (Financial Times) and the Irish Stock exchanges (Irish Times) by industry classification. The internet also provides up-to-date information on the performance of equities. The information provided is quite detailed and an investor needs to be able to read the tables that are provided. The tables typically disclose the following information:

Share information provided in financial newspapers

Pharmaceuticals and Biotech

Notes	Price	Chng	52 week high	Low	Yld	P/E	Vol. '000
Drug Co. ♣	112	−½	134	22	2.0	18.9	556
Medicine	150xd	+¾	190	135	3.2	16.8	678

(Format taken from Financial Times disclosures)

The *notes section* states the name of the company and uses playing cards symbols to provide information. A club indicates that a free annual report is available, a diamond that the company is subject to a takeover bid, merger or reorganisation, a spade indicates an unregulated investment scheme, whereas a heart indicates that the company is an overseas incorporated company. The *price column* provides the average market price of an individual share, as quoted by the market traders at 4.30 pm on the previous day. This also uses signage to provide information to the reader. When a share has the letters *xd after the price*, this signifies that the share price is ***ex-dividend*** (i.e. though a dividend has been announced, new buyers will not be entitled to the dividend). If the share price as a *(#) symbol* after it, this means that trading in the share is suspended and the price disclosed is the price before suspension. The *Chng column* details the *price change* in the 24 hours ending at 4.30pm yesterday. The *52-week high and low columns* highlight the range in price movements over the past 52 weeks by disclosing the highest and lowest prices recorded for the shares.

The *Yld column* discloses the **dividend yield** on the share. It signifies the percentage dividend return on the share (gross dividend divided by current market share price). The *P/E column* provides information on the **price-earnings ratio**. This ratio provides an indication of the number of times the market price of the share covers the earnings made per share. It provides an indication of market confidence and the higher the price-earnings ratio, the happier investors are with the company's performance, as they are paying a higher price for the company's earnings, relative to companies that report a lower price-earnings ratio. Finally, the *vol. column* reports the turnover in shares in the previous day, rounded to the nearest thousand. If a dash appears in this column, this means that there either was no trading the previous day, or the information is not available.

Gilts

Gilts are another name for government issued bonds. These investments typically have a fixed interest rate, with a set capital repayment at the end of a pre-agreed term. Gilts are regarded as being **risk-free investments** as the return is guaranteed by the government. The return earned on gilts is regarded as revenue income by the tax authorities, not capital gains. Therefore, the demand for gilts is impacted on by changes in tax rates. Individuals can purchase gilts through their bank, through the **Bank of England's Brokerage Service Direct** (UK gilts only), or through a stockbroker (UK and the ROI). Specialist stockbrokers who trade in gilts are known as **Gilt Edged Market Makers**. Information on the performance of gilts can be obtained from the financial press (as discussed under equity above) and the internet.

Bonds

Bonds are corporate issued debt that can be purchased by investors. Bonds are typically redeemable, or irredeemable. **Redeemable bonds** normally have a maturity of between seven and 30 years, though the period can be shorter or longer. **Irredeemable bonds** do not have a maturity date; though commonly can be redeemed at the borrower's request. Bonds can be sold by way of a **public issue**, (the company will have to prepare a prospectus, apply to the stock exchange and provide financial statements to the lenders, at least annually) or by a private issue. Publicly-traded bonds are traded in the secondary market of the London Stock Exchange (UK) and in the official list of the Irish Stock Exchange (ROI). A **private issue** is normally administered by a financial intermediary. They purchase the bonds from a company and sell them to a limited number of investors. These bonds are not tradable on the secondary markets of the stock exchange, but can be traded in private deals between bond brokers.

The risk associated with investing in a particular bond depends on the strength of the underlying corporation. A good indication of bond risk can be obtained from the **bond's credit rating**, which is usually performed by *Moody's*; *Standard and Poor's* and *Fitch IBCA*. Companies with publicly-traded bonds are required to keep their credit rating up-to-date. Bonds are usually given a credit rating which ranks from a triple A score (strongest) to a D which stands for Default (some only rate as far as Bbb). There are varying ratings between these scores including AA, A, BBB, BB, B, C and so on. Anything graded BBB or above is considered to have hit the **investment grade** and any bond rated below BBB is regarded as being a **junk bond**. Junk bonds are considered to be risky investments.

Like gilts, the return earned on bonds is considered by the tax authorities to be revenue income. Bond values are negatively correlated with changes in the bank base rate. When interest rates rise, the value of bonds fall, as the coupon (interest) attached to the bond is usually fixed. Like gilts, an individual can purchase bonds through their bank, through the Bank of England's Brokerage Service Direct (UK bonds only), or through a stockbroker (specialist stockbrokers who trade in gilts are known as *Bond Market Makers*). Information on the performance of bonds can be obtained from the financial press (as discussed under equity) and the internet.

Property

Two major decisions face an investor when the decision is taken to invest in property. The first involves selecting a property, the second financing the investment. *Property investment* involves a major capital outlay. The individual purchasing the property usually requires debt to finance the purchase.

Which property?

Buy-to-let property investment

An individual might choose to purchase a property for *buy-to-let* purposes. When individuals purchase buy-to-let properties they usually expect the rent from the property to exceed the costs of the property (costs include all running, management and finance costs) and to provide a yearly surplus. In addition, capital appreciation is expected.

When selecting a buy-to-let property, an individual should be advised to choose a property based on its price, the quality of the location, its condition, funds required to make it rentable, the availability of local amenities and facilities (for example, schools, leisure centres, play areas, shops), closeness to public transport and expected maintenance. For example, large gardens are attractive to tenants; however, they require high maintenance. It is likely that a large garden will not add to the rental premium that can be obtained from a property; however, the costs of maintenance will increase (landlords are usually responsible for the upkeep of the external parts of a property, with tenants being responsible for the upkeep of the internal parts of the property).

There is also a high chance that the property will not be rented for several months, if a tenant is to leave. Additional repair costs also usually have to be incurred as tenants rarely return the property in the condition they received it in.

Mortgage lenders may restrict the type of property an individual can purchase. For example, they may insist that the property has a fire escape or one kitchen (so that the property is not converted into bed-sits).

The **management of a property** can be taken on by the individual themselves, or can be contracted to a letting agency. These typically charge 10 to 15% of the rent for managing the property (including finding and vetting tenants, collecting rent and dealing with repairs – with the cost of repairs and maintenance not forming part of the commission, being extra). Care should be taken when setting up the agreement with a letting agency. The timing of rent reimbursements should be agreed up front. Letting agents can hold on to rent for a long time before reimbursing it, if the terms are not stipulated in advance. It should be policy for the letting agent to gain permission to incur certain costs and to prove that they are using a competitive source for the repairs. All rentals should be backed up using a legal rental agreement, which should be renewed yearly.

The net income from a buy-to-let property is subject to income tax and any capital growth in the value of the property is subject to capital gains tax.

Commercial property investment

Private investors can also invest in **commercial property**. As the amounts involved are typically very large this type of investment is usually only possible through collective funds such as unit trusts. Most investment, pension and insurance companies own commercial properties and several partnerships purchase offices using a '**self investment pension plan**'.

Other property investment: second home

Other investments in property might include purchasing a **second home** or a **property overseas**. Second homes are not usually rented; hence have a direct impact on an individual's monthly cash position. Second homes usually have fixed costs that have to be covered, such as ground rent, water rates, rates (NI), insurance, maintenance and utility costs. These costs are regarded as personal costs. The income to be made on a second home is usually the capital gain on the property. The tax authorities will only accept one property as the main residential property, so it is important to inform them within two years of the purchase of the second property, which one should be regarded as the main residence. The choice should be the most tax efficient choice. The property with the highest expected capital gains should be classified as the main residence (capital gains on a person's main residence are tax-free).

Other property investment: property abroad

When purchasing a second home overseas, the issues to be faced are the same as those facing properties purchased in Ireland, or in the UK, though in addition there is the added complication of having to get to know and to comply with local laws, taxes and currency fluctuations. Rent on a foreign property (net of expenses) and any capital gain made on a sale is subject to tax in both countries (the country of the property and the country of the owner – where this is different), though the foreign tax is usually taken off the individual's tax bill for the rent or capital gain with the difference being paid to the tax authorities. Though attractive gains are possible from investing in property overseas, the risks are greater (as are the costs), than the risks associated with investing in the local property market. It is advisable to obtain legal and taxation advice from an expert who resides in the country where the property is located. This advice should cover the local land laws (in Spain many individuals saw their holdings diminished as the local Spanish authorities took back land) and inheritance laws (in Spain the law determines how an estate should be divided, not an individual's will).

Type of ownership

Properties are usually of two types – freehold and leasehold. **Freehold** property means that the property and the land on which the property is situated forms the total property. **Leasehold** on the other hand involves purchasing the right to lease the buildings and gardens that are on the land for a set period of time. The investor becomes a lessee. The lease period of leasehold properties typically range from 99 years to 999 years. When the lease expires the right to use the property reverts to the lessor (the legal owner).

FINANCING PROPERTY INVESTMENT

Debt

Most properties are purchased using a mortgage. A *mortgage* is a long-term *secured loan* which allows the lender to have a legal charge encumbered on the property. The legally binding contract which sets out the terms and conditions of the loan and the restrictive covenants that the purchaser has to adhere to is called a *mortgage deed*.

Typical contents of a mortgage deed

1. The address of the property subject to the mortgage.
2. The names of the purchaser/s and the lender.
3. The amount being loaned, the set-up fees, repayment amounts, how they are calculated and the interest rate and type.
4. The granting of the legal charge over the property (the property deeds are usually retained by the bank).
5. The minimum insurance requirements and restrictions/conditions on the alterations that can happen to the property, or restrictions/conditions on how the property can be used by the purchaser. The lender usually insists that the purchaser keeps the property in a good state of repair, so that its value is not diminished and their security put at risk.
6. The steps that will be taken if the agreement is breached.
7. The purchaser's signature to confirm that they have received the loan and agree to the conditions.

Lender's perspective

Mortgage debt on property is relatively low-risk for lenders as property values typically increase, making the security stronger over time. As the lender has a *legal charge* over the property this means that they have to be repaid out of the proceeds of the property first and in addition, because the loan is **secured**, the lender can force the sale of the property if the conditions of the mortgage deed are not adhered to. In general lending institutions have a number of set criteria which they apply when deciding on whether to give a mortgage or not. The most common criteria applied by financial institutions are as follows:

Mortgage lending criteria

1. *General criteria:* Lending institutions will be interested in the credit standing of the borrower, the reputation of the borrower, the relationship they have had with the borrower in the past (for example, have they complied with all prior loan agreements), the proportion of funds being contributed by the borrower, the amount of debt already being serviced by the borrower, the amount of equity amassed by the borrower and the security on offer.

2. *The loan-to-value ratio:* How much of the investment is being contributed by the purchaser and how much is being contributed by the bank. A low '**loan-to-value ratio**' is seen as being less risky. Typical ratios range from 75% to 90%, though may amount to over 100% wherein the lender is providing additional finance for the purchaser to take payment breaks, to pay stamp duty, refurbish the property. Mortgages of over 100% are no longer available due to the current credit climate as banks are experiencing capital rationing and are less willing to increase their exposure to credit risk by providing loans that are not 100% secured by a property.

3. *The ratio of '**loan size-to-income**':* Traditionally this was set at about three times an individuals gross salary or 2.5 times a couple's gross salary (or three times the higher salary plus two times the lower salary), less other debt commitments. In recent years a higher multiple of four or five times, has become quite common. However, the downturn in the subprime market has caused lending institutions to

tighten their lending criteria and the traditional more restrictive multiples have become the norm again.

4. *The percentage of net income required to service the loan*: Lending institutions normally place a cap on the percentage of an individual's net income that should go towards paying off the debt. This is normally between 30% and 35%. This cap will restrict the repayment amount which will either restrict the amount of debt that the individual can obtain, or increase the acceptable term of the loan.

5. *Evidence*: A lending institution will typically wish to see sight of at least three month's pay slips (or the financial statements for two years), and three month's bank statements (including the most recent statements) from all bank accounts. The mortgage process usually involves a lengthy interview at which all these details are recorded and conditions, such as having house insurance, mortgage protection insurance, etc. are discussed.

Individual's (borrower's) perspective

From an individual's perspective, the mortgage decision should factor in the individual's liquidity, age and health (income generating ability and longevity), income (stability and variation) and how the investment and mortgage fit in with the individual's overall financial plan and their financial objectives. The wealthier and more cash rich an individual, the more likely they are to get the best deal to cater for their needs.

Types of mortgage

There are typically two different types of mortgage: repayment and interest only. A **repayment mortgage** involves an individual typically paying a pre-agreed monthly repayment for a set period of time (this will depend on the age of the individual, their financial aim in respect of the mortgage and their ability to meet the repayments). The repayment includes the month's interest and a portion of the capital. At the start of the mortgage most of the repayment is interest. Over time as the outstanding debt balance reduces, the capital element of each repayment increases and the interest portion reduces. The following equation can be used to determine the monthly repayment, given the interest rate and term of the mortgage:

$$P = \frac{M \times r}{1 - (1/(1 + r)^t)}$$

Where P is the periodic payment, M is the initial size of the mortgage, t is the number of payments and r is the periodic interest rate (the annual interest rate divided by the number of payments per year).

WORKED EXAMPLE 1   (Repayment mortgages)

Alex wants to borrow €/£250,000 to purchase a property. She wants a repayment mortgage. Her bank can offer an interest rate of 6%. This is competitive and Alex is very interested. She is thinking about paying the mortgage off in 20 years, though may have to agree to 25 years.

Required
As a trainee in the bank you have been asked to determine the monthly repayments required to pay off the €/£250,000, assuming the mortgage term is:

 a) 20 years
 b) 25 years
 c) Show the pattern of interest and capital repayments for the first five years assuming the 20 year option is taken.

Solution
a) The periodic payment can be calculated using the following formula:

$$P = \frac{M \times r}{1 - (1/(1 + r)^t)}$$

Where P is the periodic payment (to find)
M is the initial size of the mortgage (€/£250,000)
t is the number of payments 240 (20 × 12)
r, the periodic interest rate, is 0.5% (6%/12)

Therefore

$$P = \frac{€/£250,000 \times 0.005}{1 - (1/(1 + 0.005)^{240})}$$

$$P = €/£1,791.08$$

b) Where P is the periodic payment (to find)
M is the initial size of the mortgage (€/£250,000)
t is the number of payments 300 (25 × 12)
r, the periodic interest rate, is 0.5% (6%/12)

Therefore

$$P = \frac{€/£250,000 \times 0.005}{1 - (1/(1 + 0.005)^{300})}$$

$$P = €/£1,610.75$$

c)

Year	Opening balance €/£	Interest (6%) €/£	Capital repayment €/£	Closing balance €/£
1	250,000.00	15,000.00[1]	6,492.96[2]	243,507.04[3]
2	243,507.04	14,610.42	6,882.54	236,624.50
3	236,624.50	14,197.47	7,295.49	229,329.01
4	229,329.01	13,759.74	7,733.22	221,595.79
5	221,595.79	13,295.75	8,197.21	213,398.58

1. The interest for the year is calculated on the opening balance:
   €/£250,000 × 6%
2. The capital repayment is €/£6,492.96 ((€/£1,791.08 × 12) −
   €/£15,000)
3. The closing balance is €/£243,507.04 (€/£250,000 − €/£6,492.96)

As can be seen from the solution to part c) above the yearly repayment remains the same at €/£21,492.96 (€/£1,791.08 x 12), but the proportion of this that goes to pay interest on the mortgage reduces and the capital amount increases each year.

The alternative type of mortgage is the ***interest only mortgage***. As the name stipulates, the repayment is interest only. The capital amount does not reduce over the life of the loan. If Alex (above example) were to opt for an interest-only mortgage then her yearly repayments would be €/£15,000 or €/£1,250 per month (€/£15,000/12). Individuals might opt for an interest only mortgage for an initial period of time for liquidity reasons. When an individual purchases a new property there are many costs, the individual may wish to reduce their debt servicing costs in the initial period so that they have sufficient liquid cash to cover the initial bills.

In the 1980s and early 1990s many individuals took out ***endowment mortgages***. These mortgages were interest-only mortgages with a set monthly amount also being directed into an endowment investment fund. The theory being that the endowment fund would increase in value and would be of sufficient size by the end of the loan period to repay the capital balance outstanding. In most cases these mortgages did not provide sufficient funds to repay the capital. Individuals had to increase their contributions, and in many cases the endowment fund still did not cover the outstanding loan. Many financial advisers were considered to have mis-sold the mortgages and millions of pounds were paid out in compensation. The following equation can be used to determine the amount to pay into an endowment type mortgage to ensure that the policy matures with sufficient funds to cover the mortgage liability:

$$M = \frac{p((1 + y)t - 1)}{y}$$

Where M is the target maturity amount, p is the periodic payment, t is the number of periods and y is the rate of return expected to be earned by the fund. The target maturity fund will only be achieved if the fund earns the expected rate of return.

WORKED EXAMPLE   (Endowment mortgages)

Alex wants to borrow €/£250,000 to purchase a property. She wants an endowment mortgage. Her bank can offer her the €/£250,000 at an interest rate of 6% and an endowment product which is expected to earn a return of 8%. She is thinking about paying the mortgage off in 20 years, though may have to agree to 25 years.

Required

As a trainee in the bank you have been asked to determine the monthly repayments required to pay the interest and to pay into the endowment fund so that it will have a maturity value of €/£250,000, assuming the mortgage term is:

   a)   20 years
   b)   25 years

Solution

a) The interest payment each year to the bank will be €/£1,250 ((€/£250,000 x 6%)/12).

   The periodic payment to the endowment can be calculated using the following formula:

$$M = \frac{p((1 + y)t - 1)}{y}$$

Where

M, the target maturity amount, is €/£250,000
p is the periodic payment (to find)
t, the number of periods, is 20
and y, the rate of return expected to be earned by the fund, is 8%.

$$€/£250,000 = \frac{p((1 + 0.08)^{20} - 1)}{0.08}$$

$$€/£250,000 = p \times 45.762$$

$$€/£250,000/45.762 = p$$

$$€/£5,463.05 = p$$

Therefore the monthly payment to the endowment policy will be €/£455.25 (€/£5,463.05/12).

The total monthly payment will be €/£1,705.25 (€/£1,250 + €/£455.25)

b) Where p is the periodic payment (to find)

M is the initial size of the mortgage (€/£250,000)

t is the number of payments 25

r, the periodic interest rate, is 8%

Therefore

$$€/£250,000 = \frac{p((1 + 0.08)^{25} - 1)}{0.08}$$

$$€/£250,000 = p \times 73.106$$

$$€/£250,000/73.106 = p$$

$$€/£3,419.69 = p$$

Therefore the monthly payment to the endowment policy will be €/£284.97 (€/£3,419.69/12).

The total monthly payment will be €/£1,534.97 (€/£1,250 = €/£284.97)

A similar option which is available at the moment is called a **lifestyle fund**. Under this fund the contributions in the early stages of the mortgage are invested in equity, as the investment reaches maturity, the funds are transferred into bonds, finally into deposit accounts – so that the final balance cannot be affected by a fall in the equity markets shortly before the fund is to mature.

MORTGAGE TERMS: INTEREST RATES

Mortgage lenders have to quote their interest rates as APRs or EAR (Equivalant Annual Rates). This allows comparison across financial institutions. However, most financial institutions use other costs to gain revenues. For example, a mortgage lender may charge a set-up fee, they may insist that their house insurance product is purchased, or they may factor in a redemption fee.

There are two main types of interest rate: fixed-rate and variable-rate. **Fixed-rate mortgages** fix the interest rate being charged by the lending institution for a set period of time (typically one to two years, though terms of up to ten years have been used in the past). This type of mortgage suits an individual who has a high debt-to-income ratio. They will be more risk adverse and will be attracted to this type of mortgage as it hedges their exposure against increases in interest rates. This will also be seen as attractive to an individual who believes that interest rates will increase. These mortgages normally involve a high redemption penalty if the mortgage is redeemed within a specified period of time.

In a *variable-rate mortgage* the interest charged is usually pegged to the bank's base rate, (in the ROI, banks' base rates are pegged to the European Central Bank base rate – Euribor; in the UK, banks' base rates are pegged to the Bank of England base rate), or some other base rate. Therefore, when the base rate increases by 0.25%, so does the interest being charged on the mortgage. This product is commonly referred to as a '*tracker mortgage*'.

MORTGAGE TERMS: INTRODUCTORY OFFERS

To attract mortgage customers, most financial institutions who provide mortgages offer introductory inducements. For example, the majority of variable rate/tracker mortgages come with an introductory discount on their variable rate. This discount is typically between 0.5% and 3% and ranges for a period of between six months and two years. Like fixed rate mortgages, a redemption fee will be payable if the mortgage is altered/repaid within a fixed period of time. In addition to this, it is possible that the lender will provide some cash back, or pay legal fees. These incentives are attractive for individuals who wish to keep the cash outflows to a minimum in the initial years. The incentives are usually repayable if the loan were to be redeemed within a specified term (usually two to five years).

OTHER MORTGAGE PRODUCTS

The competition between lending institutions has resulted in a variety of types of mortgage products being available. The most commonly sourced types are now outlined briefly.

Cap and collar mortgages

Cap and collar mortgages combine the benefit of having interest rate risk hedged as under a fixed-rate mortgage and allowing the borrower to benefit, to an extent, when interest rates fall as under a variable-rate mortgage. The interest rate on this product moves freely in line with the bank's base rate between the two limits. The **cap** is the predetermined upper interest rate limit and the **collar** is the lower interest rate limit. If mortgage rates fall below the predetermined collar level, the lender benefits from the arrangement; if the rates rise above the cap level, the borrower benefits.

Offset mortgage

An **offset mortgage** involves pooling an individual's mortgage account with their savings and current accounts into one pot for the purpose of determining the interest to be charged for the period. The individual bank accounts are separate and have their own unique account number. The savings and current accounts do not earn interest, as their daily balances are used to save interest on the mortgage amount. The arrangement can be set up to have a fixed repayment, which means that the additional repayment caused by the interest saving will be used to repay the capital – hence the mortgage debt will be paid off quicker, or the monthly mortgage repayment could be reduced by the amount of interest saved. When an individual has liquidity needs the latter option is likely to be preferable. This product usually allows capital repayments to be made at any time. On the downside this product typically incurs a higher interest rate relative to straightforward variable-rate mortgages.

Current account mortgages

Current account mortgages are similar to offset mortgages except there is only one account that has an overall lending limit. The interest is charged on the amount borrowed. When this type of mortgage is being utilised, it would make sense not to have a separate deposit account, but to lodge all funds in the current account, to reduce the net debt.

Flexible mortgage

A *flexible mortgage* allows variation in the repayment schedule (there will be limits), additional capital draw-downs (to a limit) and the ability to make capital repayments without incurring a penalty (to a limit).

Shared appreciation mortgages

A further product that is available and is attractive to first time buyers who cannot afford to purchase their own property, or to elderly people who wish to access some of the equity built up in their property is *shared appreciation mortgages*. These mortgages effectively allow an individual to purchase a portion of their home with an external body purchasing the remainder. The monthly repayments include a mortgage repayment and a rent for the portion that is not owned. The rent is paid to the other owner. In NI the scheme is supported by the government and is administered by the Co-ownership Housing Association Scheme.

When the individual wishes to purchase the remainder of their property at some future date, it is the capital value at that date that is applied to determine the price. There may also be issues in respect of improvements. The individual may undertake improvements which add value to the property as a whole, yet will still have to purchase the remainder at the higher market value.

RE-MORTGAGING

Most individuals are advised to re-mortgage their property as soon as the lock-in period is over. The *lock-in period* is a condition of most mortgages. The individual obtaining the mortgage agrees to meet the repayment terms in full during this period. It is a fixed term, typically the first two, three or five years of a mortgage. Re-mortgaging within the lock-in period can result in heavy penalties which reduce the attractiveness of re-mortgaging. After the lock-in period an individual might be in a position to repay part of the mortgage debt (reducing the monthly cash outflow), or may wish to extend the mortgage to finance something else (mortgages are typically the cheapest form of debt). If the mortgage is being extended to pay back bad debt, this should be regarded as a short-term requirement, which the individual should aim to clear in full at the next re-mortgage. An individual should aim to clear their mortgage debt fully by the time they retire.

ROI MORTGAGE INTEREST RELIEF

Since 1 January the Irish Government has allowed 20% mortgage interest Tax Relief at Source (TRS). This is given by the lender either as a reduced mortgage payment or as a credit to the individual's account. This tax relief only applies to mortgage debt that is secured on an individual's main residence, so long as it is located in the ROI. From 1 January 2008 the ceiling for claiming relief on interest was set at €10,000 for a single first time buyer or €20,000 for a married couple or a widowed individual who are classed as first time buyers. This equates to cash savings of €2,000 for an individual or €4,000 for a married couple on their mortgage repayments. The relief at these levels is allowed in the year of purchase and the subsequent six years. The ceiling amount that interest can be claimed on for all other individuals is €3,000 for a single person and €6,000 for a married couple, or a widowed individual. This equates to cash savings of €600 for an individual or €1,200 for a married couple on their mortgage repayments.

COLLECTIVE FUNDS (IN BRIEF)

Collective funds, otherwise known as **mutual funds, managed funds,** or just simply **funds**, are investment vehicles that combine a wide range of assets to create a diversified investment portfolio. They allow individuals to participate in a wider range of investments than they would, were they to invest in the underlying assets on an individual basis.

The most common types of collective funds are unit trusts, investment trusts and life assurance funds. These products are invested in by many investment companies, including pension companies.

Unit trusts

Unit trusts are 'open ended' investments that have a specific aim. The term **'open ended'** means that the trust managers can create or cancel units depending on demand for the units. The value of the units is linked to the value of the underlying portfolio of asset investments which make up the fund. The underlying assets are predominately property, equity and bonds. The returns on these different classes of asset are considered to be negatively correlated and are assumed to hedge the overall return of the trust.

Unless part of a government tax break scheme, unit trust gains are subject to capital gains tax when they are sold/redeemed.

Investment trusts

Investment trusts are usually British companies that are listed on the London Stock Exchange. They specialise in investing in equity shares (quoted and unquoted) and in other investment trusts both in the UK and overseas. An investment in these companies is possible by buying their shares on the stock exchange. This means that the value of this investment is influenced by the performance of the underlying equity assets that are held by the investment trust company and by demand for the company's shares in the market. If they are trading at an amount which is below the value of the underlying company assets then they are more attractive to an investor than if they were trading at a value which is greater than the value of the underlying assets.

Like unit trusts, gains on investment trust shares that are sold are subject to capital gains tax, unless they are included in a Government tax break scheme.

Life insurance investment bonds

Life insurance investment bonds invest in similar types of assets to those invested in by investment trusts, though are sold for a specified term (this is why they are referred to as 'bonds'). They are similar to unit trusts in their make-up. An individual who invests in the life insurance bond gets a set number of units which reflect the value of the underlying assets. However, a portion of the investment is used to provide life cover. The taxation of these investments is complicated. As this investment is being covered only very briefly in this text, the author recommends that any potential investor investigates the tax consequences very carefully. In simple terms, fund holders pay the income tax and capital gains tax on the gains made on the underlying investments at the lower rate of tax. The bonds can be either regarded as qualifying or non-qualifying by Revenue and Customs/Revenue Commissioners. On maturity, a *qualifying* policy has no further tax to pay. However, higher-rate tax payers who have invested in a *non-qualifying* policy may have to pay additional tax on maturity. Steps can be taken to manage/reduce the potential liability. **Endowment mortgage policies** are examples of qualifying life assurance investment bonds.

Collective funds can be **'with profits'** (wherein the policyholder is able to reap the benefits of the returns made by all the company's businesses – or the losses), **'protected funds'** or **'guaranteed funds'**. Protected or guaranteed funds are usually linked to an index. The growth rate advertised may be guaranteed, but the capital value is not – for example a total return of 20% over three years may be guaranteed, but the capital value might fall by 70%. In this case the guaranteed return is 20% of the 30% remaining capital balance. The capital loss more than outweighs the guaranteed return earned!

TANGIBLE ASSETS

Many investors choose to purchase tangible assets as part of their investment portfolio. Assets typically invested in include artwork, wine, forestry, antiques and classic cars. Any collectable item can have the potential to result in gains. The gains may be subject to capital gains tax, duty and value added tax (VAT). In each instance, the investor should clarify the current taxation situation (across all the taxes) before investing. In addition to the financial reward, an individual can also gain pleasure out of having the item (for example, art, antiques, gold or wine) or can feel satisfaction from the act of promoting environmentally friendly activities (if purchasing/creating forests). The advantages and disadvantages of some of the main tangible asset investments are now outlined.

Art/photography/antiques

The value of artwork, photographs and antiques can rise and fall in value. Over the past 20 years, investments in these items have, if carefully selected, outperformed the markets (A Bawden, 2002). An excellent example is the recent sale by actor Hugh Grant of his Andy Warhol 1963 painting of Elizabeth Taylor, called 'Liz (coloured Liz)'. Hugh Grant purchased the painting in Sotheby's in 2001 for a reported $3.6 million (Ivory, 2007) and sold it in November 2007 for $23.7 million (the actor is reported to have received around $21 million after commission (circa 12%)).

Investing in art/photography/antiques can be risky; the value of an item may fall in line with the world economy (the credit crunch in America may prolong, the current oil price has reached an all time high and may rise higher); an investor may purchase a fake; an investor may pay over the odds for the item at the time of purchase because of lack of knowledge. In addition, there are the high costs that are involved with buying, insuring, housing the items securely, transporting and selling the items. Auction houses can charge up to 20% of the sale value for commission and insurance while the item is on their premises.

Gold and gemstones

There is a readily available market for gold and over the period from mid 2007 to March 2008, the price of gold reached an all-time high. Gold is sometimes used to hedge an investment portfolio as its value is usually negatively correlated to the performance of the equity markets. Investment in gemstones can also be lucrative, but this market is attractive to fraudsters and care needs to be taken if gemstones are being considered for an individual's investment portfolio.

Wine

Sometimes referred to as **liquid gold**, investing in wine has become more attractive, though is risky for the uninformed individual. There are win-win stories that stimulate the interest of the investing community, such as the purchase of a case of 'Le Pin' for €/£150 in 1982 being worth over €/£18,000 in today's market (Heartwood, 2006); however, there are many pitfalls. Firstly, only certain types of wine are regarded as investments by the market. The Bordeaux region of France comprises about 94.41% of the *Liv-ex 100 index* (the fine wine benchmark index). Bordeaux (Red) wine accounts for 93.4% with Bordeaux (White) accounting for 1.01% of the Liv-ex 100 index value. The index rose by 40% in value over the year to 31 December 2007 (www.**liv-ex**.com, accessed January 2008). Skilled knowledge of wine is vital for successful investment. The value of wine is influenced by vintage, chateau, classification system, taste and longevity, quantity produced, storage conditions and the ongoing cost of maintenance. In addition, the value of wine is suscepti-ble to trends. It is currently fashionable to invest in wine, but this may change in the future. *Fine wine* is classed as a wasting asset by Revenue and Customs/Revenue Commis-sioners, hence is not subject to capital gains tax. The gains on wine are subject to capital gains tax in some instances – this is where Revenue and Customs/Revenue Commission-ers consider a wine's life to be greater than 50 years, or they decide it is a business asset on the grounds that it is being used for trade.

Forestry

Investing in forestry is attractive in the UK because it is sup-ported by the UK Government as part of their environmen-tal policy. To this end, the UK Government does not charge capital gains tax on the increase in value of the tree crop, if sold (though the increase in value of the underlying land is taxable). They do not charge inheritance tax on the value of the forest (so long as held for two years prior to death) and the sale of felled timber is free from income tax and capital gains tax. Forestry grants are not taxable (though the annual grant receivable from the Farm Woodland Premium Scheme is taxable). On the downside a forest takes over 20 years to mature (this depends on the type of tree, with oak trees tak-ing over 100 years to mature) and is subject to damage by nature (fire, winds and disease).

CONCLUSION

Long-term investments should form part of every individu-al's financial plan. An individual is more likely to earn higher returns from long-term investments than from short-term investments. Indeed, many short-term investments can actually damage an individual's wealth as the return earned may not exceed inflation. Yet purchasing long-term investments has disadvantages, as funds are locked away and heavy penalties are incurred if the investments are cashed earlier than planned. In some instances, potentially lucrative long-term investments can be loss making in the short term. The equity market is a good example. If an individual were to invest funds in shares for a six-month period, they run the chance of making a loss, whereas if they were to purchase a balanced portfolio of shares for 20 years, it is more likely that good returns would be made. The risk-return relationship is also relevant. The equity markets are regarded as risky, hence a strong return is possible, as is a loss.

Individuals should always ensure that sufficient liquidity is retained, yet try to ensure that funds are not invested inefficiently – for example, kept in low-return bank accounts.

Most individuals, at some stage in their life, purchase their own home. This is a long-term investment and should be properly planned for. There is a variety of mortgage products and this chapter has introduced a number of the more common types. Whether to opt for a repayment or endowment type mortgage with either a fixed or variable rate of interest will depend on individuals' preference and views on how the equity markets will perform and how interest rates will move.

KEY TERMS

Advisory arrangement
Bank of England's
   Brokerage Service Direct
Bond market makers
Bonds
Buy-to-let properties
Cap and collar mortgages
Capital bonds
Collective funds
Commercial property
Contracted out
Current account mortgage

Discretionary arrangement
Diversified portfolio of
   investments
Dividend yield
Endowment mortgage
Ex-dividend
Execution only service
Fine wine
Fixed-rate mortgage
Flexible mortgage
Freehold property
Gilt edged market makers

Gilts
Guaranteed funds
High-risk investments
Interest only mortgage
Investment grade
Investment bonds
Investment decision
Investment grade
Investment trusts
Investment units
Irredeemable bonds
Junk bond
Leasehold property
Legal charge
Life insurance investment
  bond
Lifestyle fund
Liv-ex 100 index
Loan-to-value ratio
Loan-size-to-income ratio
Lock-in period
Low-risk investments
Managed funds
Mutual funds
Modest-risk investments
Mortgage
Mortgage deed
Negatively correlated

No-risk investments
Offset mortgage
Overseas property
Open ended
Price-earnings ratio
Private issue
Property investment
Protected funds
Public issue
Redeemable bonds
Relatively-high-risk
  investment
Repayment mortgage
Risk-free investments
Risk-return relationship
Second home
Secured loan
Self-invested pension plan
Self-liquidating
  investments
Self-select service
Shared appreciation
  mortgage
Tracker mortgage
Unit trusts
Variable rate mortgage
Wine
With profits

WEBSITES THAT MAY BE OF USE

There are many sites that are geared towards giving advice on debt management. A couple have been highlighted here, though a Google search would provide you with a wealth of information.

For information on purchasing properties through co-ownership visit:
http://www.co-ownership.org/

For information on collective funds visit:
http://www.occ.treas.gov/handbook/ciffinal.pdf

Information on personal finance products in the ROI can be obtained from the following website:
http://www.itsyourmoney.ie/

Information on personal finance products in NI can be obtained from the following
http://www.moneymadeclear.fsa.gov.uk/

REVIEW QUESTIONS

(Answers to review questions are provided in Appendix three)

1. What are the differences between bonds and equity shares?
2. What is a risk-free investment?
3. Geoffrey requires a mortgage facility of €/£280,000 to purchase a property. He would like to be able to repay this over 15 years. He is wondering how much the monthly repayment would be, given that interest rates on this type of product are currently about 5%.

Required

   a) Calculate the expected monthly repayment for Geoffrey.

4. Geoffrey is also looking at an endowment type mortgage. He has been told that funds invested are currently earning 7%. The mortgage costs 5%. He feels that he would be better off, were he to opt for the endowment mortgage.

Required

   a) Calculate the expected monthly repayment for Geoffrey.
   b) What factors should Geoffrey take into consideration when deciding on whether to opt for a repayment or an endowment type mortgage?
5. List three differences between unit trusts and investment trusts.
6. What are the benefits of investing in collective fund products from an investor's viewpoint?

CHAPTER 9

PENSIONS

Learning Objectives

Upon completion of this chapter, readers should be able to:

- Explain the meaning of the key terms listed at the end of the chapter;
- Discuss the merits of having a pension;
- Describe the way the public/state pension works in your jurisdiction;
- Explain the difference between a public/state and a private pension;
- Explain the difference between a personal and an occupational pension scheme;
- Explain the difference between a defined contribution and a defined benefit pension scheme; and
- Detail how tax relief is given on pensions in your jurisdiction.

INTRODUCTION

Most young people look towards retirement as a positive thing, imagining golf, holidays and a life of comfort. A life where they are able to do all those things that they could not do because of work. However, many individuals who are in their 40s, 50s and early 60s are anxious about retirement. To them retirement means withdrawing from active working life. This means leaving their occupation, their status, their position and their link to the working social network. There is also the realisation that their income level will fall and there is uncertainty as to how they will be able to finance their current lifestyle. Many have to accept a reduction in lifestyle.

The problem has been accentuated by the increase in the longevity of individuals, the inability of the government to finance current public pension expectations and the reduction in the number of company defined benefit schemes.

LONGEVITY OF INDIVIDUALS

The average age of a person born in 1900 was 47, whereas the Faculty of Actuaries estimate that males aged 65 in 2002 can expect to live until they are 81 years of age (on average); whereas females, aged 65 in 2002, have an average life expectancy of 84 years. This is expected to increase by a further three to four years by 2020. Therefore, some individuals may be in retirement for periods that equal the period of time they spent working. This means that financing retirement is a growing problem.

PENSIONS

Pensions are monies that are paid to an individual or their spouse, usually on retirement, or when they reach retirement age. There are two types of pension: state pensions and private pensions. Both pensions operate in a different manner. State pensions are considered first.

STATE PENSIONS (ROI)

A common misconception individuals have, is that when they pay their *pay related social insurance (PRSI),* a portion is put aside to cover their pension. This is not the case. The Irish Government adopts a *'pay-as-you-go' policy.* Current employed individuals' PRSI contributions pay for current pension expenditure. There are two state pensions available in the ROI: the contributory pension and the non-contributory pension.

Contributory state pension

At the time of writing the maximum *contributory state pension*[1] of €223.30 per week for an individual, topped up by a further €200 for a qualified adult i.e. partner/spouse, is available to any individual who is aged 66 or over and who has paid at least 260 weekly full-rate employment contributions and a yearly average of at least 48 paid or credited weekly full-rate contributions from 1979 to the end of the tax year when the individual reaches 66 years of age. The 260 weekly full-rate employment contributions is increasing to 520 for individuals who reach pension age on or after 6 April 2012. At the time of writing a minimum contributory state pension (€111.70 per week for an individual topped up by a further

---

[1] SW 118 'State Pension (Transition) and State Pension (Contributory) – 2008 rates.

€100 for a qualified corrected adult i.e. partner spouse: 2008 rates) is available to any person who paid a yearly average of ten weekly full-rate contributions (full-rate contributions are PRSI contributions at classes A, E, F, G, H and N and class S for self-employed individuals).

Transition state pension

A *transition state pension* is available to persons who are 65. This is available for just one year and is only available to people who are retired or who earn less than €38 per week[2] and satisfy certain social security contribution conditions (same as those outlined above for contributory pensions). Individuals automatically transfer to the contributory pension when they reach the age of 66. It is worth noting that people who are 66 can take up employment again, without suffering a loss in their contributory pension. The contributory pension for the individual who built up the contributions is not means-tested, though the pension for any related qualifying adult may be reduced, as their pension is means-tested.

Non-contributory state pension

The *non-contributory state pension* is a means-tested pension that is available to all ROI habitual residents, who are over 66, who have a valid personal public service number and who satisfy a means test. The less an individual has, the higher the non-contributory state pension that is receivable. Any individual who has other cash income, income from employment of over €200, income from self-employment, or capital assets such as property (except for the individual's permanent residence), investments or savings, will have their non-contributory state pension reduced.

The individual's capital value is converted to reflect a weekly income. Each €1,000 is converted to a euro income equivalent. The first €20,000 of capital is free, the next €10,000 is considered to equate to a weekly income of €10 (€1 for each €1,000 held above the threshold), the next band

---

[2] SW 118 'State Pension (Transition) and State Pension (Contributory) – 2008 rates.

of €10,000 is converted at the rate of €2 for every €1,000 held, with the final band (capital held amounting to more than €40,000) considered to be equivalent to a weekly income of €4 for each €1,000 held. The maximum non-contributory state pension receivable in 2007/08 is €212 for an individual with €140.10 available for a qualifying adult who lives with the individual and who is less than 65 years of age (this increases to €212 if they also are 66 or over). This diminishes to zero where the individual is deemed to have a weekly 'means' income of over €237.50 per week[3]. The value of partner/spouse income and capital is also included when calculating the weekly means income.

WORKED EXAMPLE 1 (Non-contributory pension: ROI)

S. Moke, who is 66, has just retired. He is entitled to the non-contributory pension in the ROI. He is currently employed with a weekly income of €220, has farm income on land that he lets of €30 per week. He has €15,000 in the bank and a property worth €60,000 (this is in addition to his home).

Required
a) Provide an estimate of the non-contributory pension that S. Moke will be entitled to, given the above information.
b) You are subsequently told that S. Moke has a partner, who is aged 64. She has savings of €55,000 and has no income.

Solution
a) The starting point is to work out S. Moke's weekly means.

---

[3] Rates can be found in the publication 'SW19: Payments for Retired or Older People.

		€
Income from employment over the €200 threshold		20
Income from self-employment		30

Capital *(weekly means assessed)*

Bank	€15,000
Property	€60,000
Total	€75,000
Exemption	(€20,000)
Balance	€55,000

Assessed as:

€10,000 × €1 per €1,000	€10	
€10,000 × €2 per €1,000	€20	
€35,000 × €4 per €1,000	€140	€170
Weekly means		€220

State pension (non-contributory) per week   €19.50

(Rate obtained from SW19: Payment for Retired or Older People, 2008)

b) S. Moke has a partner who also has savings of €55,000. It is assumed that the capital is jointly owned. Therefore the new pension is:

		€
Income from employment over the €200 threshold		20
Income from self-employment		30

Capital weekly means assessed

Bank	€70,000
Property	€60,000
Total	€130,000
Assessable (1/2)	€65,000
Exemption	€20,000
Balance	€45,000

Assessed as:

€10,000 × €1 per €1,000	€10	
€10,000 × €2 per €1,000	€20	
€25,000 × €4 per €1,000	€100	€130
Weekly means		€180

State pension (non-contributory) per week   €59.50
State pension payable to the partner   €39.30

(Rates obtained from SW19: Payment for Retired or Older People, 2008)

Other benefits

Other benefits open to retired persons in the ROI include increases to the state pension (there is a living alone allowance, an age 80 allowance, a fuel allowance, an island allowance, an allowance for a qualified adult or qualified children) or other schemes for the retired (a free travel pass; an electricity, natural gas or bottled gas refill allowance; a free television licence; a free telephone allowance; a carer's allowance; or a medical card (conditions apply for most of these allowances)). As mentioned previously, retired people who are over 65 years of age are exempt from paying DIRT.

STATE PENSIONS (UK)

When the welfare state was introduced post-war in Britain (after suggestions by Beveridge in 1942), a cradle to grave approach was adopted, with the government vowing to look after its citizens from birth to death. The state pension was part of this policy and was considered to be favourable at that time. However, the state pension started to fall in value relative to the UK population's income levels in the late 1970s and limits on the amount that would be paid as a state pension were imposed in 2002 when the 'State Earnings Related Pension Scheme' was closed (discussed below). It would seem that current government policy is paving the way for further reductions in the value of state pension in the future. The most recent change is an increase in the pension age. The state pension is currently available to women who reach the age of 60 and men who reach the age of 65. The pension age for women will increase to 65 by 2020 with both limits being gradually raised to 68 by 2046. In addition, the pension amount is falling (relative to current living standards) and the UK Government is encouraging the population to take responsibility for investing in their own future.

The public pension is paid out of **national insurance contributions**. This tax provides various benefits for an individual. The individual's entitlement to the benefits depends on their prior contribution record. The benefits that can be claimed, if necessary, are weekly income benefits and some lump-sum benefits upon unemployment, maternity and disability, retirement and death.

Like in the ROI a common misconception individuals in the UK have, is that when they pay their national insurance contributions a portion is put aside to cover their pension. This is not the case. The government adopts a *'pay-as-you-go' policy*. Current employed individuals' national insurance contributions pay for current pension expenditure. In addition, the current ethos is that benefits are more **means-tested** (not **universal**), therefore employed individuals who pay higher levels of National Insurance contributions do not benefit to the same extent as they used to. Indeed, individuals who save for their retirement are actually penalised when it comes to being able to claim a pension credit. A brief synopsis of the state pension is now provided.

There are two main pensions available, both of which rise with inflation and are taxable: the basic state pension and the state second pension.

The basic state pension

The *basic state pension*, which is a flat-rate pension, is payable to a single individual at the rate of £90.70 per week for the year 2008/09[4] (this can be topped to £124.05 per week with a pension credit), or to a married couple at the rate of £145.05[5] per week for the year 2008/09 (this can be topped to £189.35 per week with a pension credit), so long as the individual contributed national insurance contributions for nine out of every ten years of their working life. Men need to have contributed for 44 years, women 39 years.

Pension credits

A *pension credit* is available to individuals who are aged over 60. It strives to ensure that individuals receive a minimum weekly income as denoted in the brackets above. Savings over £6,000 will reduce the pension credit as will most other sources of income, including the state second pension (there are some exemptions).

---

[4]This was £87.30 per week in the year 2007/08 and could have been topped to £119.05 per week with a pension credit.

[5]This was £139.60 per week in the year 2007/08 and could have been topped to £181.70 per week with a pension credit.

Second state pension

The *State Second Pension (S2P)* is an additional pension that is available to people who have paid compulsory national insurance contributions for 90% of their working life over and above those required for the basic state pension. An individual can opt to *contract out* of the state second pension and have the relevant national insurance contributions paid into a private pension scheme. The S2P replaced the *State Earnings Related Pension Scheme (SERPS)* in 2002. SERPS was established in 1978. It initially provided a pension equal to 25% of the average indexed excess earnings on which national insurance contributions are paid (over and above the amount required for the basic state pension) by an individual over their working life (this is reduced when the 90% rule is not fulfilled). Over the last two decades the SERPS pension has been reduced and eventually replaced. Pensions payable on the average excess earnings prior to 1988 still remain at 25%; however, a separate calculation is prepared for the indexed average excess earnings earned between 1988 and 2002 when the new S2P came into play. The rate used to calculate the SERP pension depends on the date at which an individual becomes a pensioner. The rate tapers from 24.5% for a person who becomes a pensioner in 2000/01 to 20% for an individual who becomes a pensioner in 2009/10. SERPS is protected so anyone who contributed national insurance contributions prior to 2002 is entitled to the SERPS state pension amount that was running at that time.

The S2P applies for national insurance contributions earned between 6 April 2002 and the 5 April 2010. Under the new scheme the indexed yearly income is split into three bands with different rates being applied to each band. The S2P gives a more generous additional State Pension to low and moderate earners, carers and people with a long-term illness or disability. By 2030 it is anticipated that the S2P will be a flat-rate additional top-up pension.

Other benefits

Retired people in the UK are also entitled to claim grants to undertake works that improve the energy efficiency of their homes and are entitled to claim a winter fuel allowance of £250 (2008/09) if over 60 years of age[6] and to claim £400, if over 80 years of age[7]. When an individual reaches the age of 60 they are entitled to a free travel pass and when they reach the age of 70 they are entitled to a free television licence. Pensioners are also entited to a reduction in council tax (Britain) and a 10% reduction in their rates bill (NI).

PRIVATE PENSIONS (UK AND THE ROI)

Non-public pension schemes operate differently to a public pension schemes. As mentioned, **public pensions** in the UK are funded from current national insurance contributions (ROI: PRSI). This means that public pensions are susceptible to changes in government policy and the economy (if the economy goes into recession, national insurance contributions fall and governments are less likely to award pension increases resulting in the value of the public pension diminishing, in real terms). There are typically two types of private pension scheme, personal schemes and company pension schemes. These are now discussed in turn.

PERSONAL PENSION SCHEMES

In a **personal pension scheme** an individual's expected pension payout is wholly dependent on:

- the specific contributions made to the pension pot;
- the performance of the administrator in the investment of the contributions over the contributing life of the individual; and
- the expected performance of the pension fund that will be purchased from the accumulated pension pot.

Personal pension funds are usually administered by financial organisations such as banks, insurance companies, unit trusts or building societies. They charge for starting up, investing and administering the pension investment (these charges are taken out of the pension funds). At retirement

---

[6]This was £200 in 2007/08.
[7]This was £300 in 2007/08.

age the built-up monies are used to purchase a separate pension fund from a pension company.

An individual's pension will be paid from this fund. A **pension fund** is a pool of assets that are established, when an individual comes of pension age, for the sole purpose of providing a pension. They are legally independent funds from the pension company and all the other funds. The format of a pension is typically:

- a cash annuity (taxable on the individual at their normal income tax rate); or
- a lump sum; or
- some combination of both.

In both the ROI and in the UK, the lump-sum is tax-free if it is less than 25% of the pension fund. The tax-free amount is further limited to 25% of the lifetime allowance where the pension fund has a fund value that is greater than the lifetime fund allowance. The **lifetime allowance** is a government set, tax-free limit, on the total value of an individual's pension fund. The value of amounts held beyond this target limit, are subject to taxation. In many instances the individual who will receive the pension has some say over the format of the pension to be received.

INDIVIDUALS WHO SHOULD CONSIDER A PERSONAL PENSION SCHEME INCLUDE:

1   Self-employed people.
2   Unemployed people who can afford to pay contributions.
3   Employees who do not have a company pension scheme (either the company does not run one, or they do not contribute to the company scheme).
4   Employees who do pay into a company pension scheme but at a low level, as their income is moderate *(NOTE: It is considered to be better to make additional voluntary contributions to the company scheme or to consider a stakeholder pension).*

The different tax treatments for pensions for both the ROI and NI are now outlined.

TAX RELIEF ON PERSONAL PENSION CONTRIBUTIONS (ROI)

In the ROI tax relief depends on an individual's age and their earnings. An individual who pays tax at the standard rate will be entitled to a tax refund of 26%[8] up to the limits outlined in the following table. A higher rate taxpayer will be entitled to relief at 43%[9]. The government pays this direct to the pension provider. The tax relief limits on yearly contributions (which apply to private and occupational pension schemes) are as follows:

Age	Percentage of earnings
Under 30 years	Up to 15% of earnings*
Aged 30 to 39 years	Up to 20% of earnings*
Aged 40 to 49 years	Up to 25% of earnings*
Aged 50 to 54 years	Up to 30% of earnings*
Aged 55 to 59 years	Up to 30% of earnings*
Aged 60 or over	Up to 40% of earnings*
Where annual earnings are capped at €262,383 (July 2007)	

The tax relief is given at source, with the pension contribution being deduced from the taxable income before the tax liability is calculated.

The maximum pension fund (from all sources) that an individual can have for tax-free status is €5.165 million (March 2007 rates). Any pension funds that exceed this limit are taxable at the rate of 41% (income tax). An individual is entitled to receive up to 25% of this lifetime allowance (€1,291,250: March 2007 rates) as a tax-free lump sum. Any lump sum payment in excess of this limit is taxable at the individual's marginal rate of tax.

The following formula is sometimes used to determine if an individual's pension scheme value is above the lifetime allowance:

---

[8]Tax relief at 20% plus PRSI relief at 6% (2007 rates)
[9]Tax relief at 41% plus PRSI relief at 2% (2007 rates)

$$LTA\% = \text{Annual pension} \times 20 + (\text{Lump sum/Lifetime allowance} \times 100)$$

The LTA% is the lifetime allowance percentage. If this equation works out at over 100% then the pension fund built-up will have exceeded the lifetime allowance percentage and a tax change will be payable on the excess.

FLEXIBLE PRIVATE RETIREMENT FUND (ROI)

The *Personal Retirement Savings Accounts (PRSAs)* is a retirement plan that is flexible, convenient and offers value for money (it has tax benefits). It is linked to an individual, hence follows that person between employments and if self-employed. When an employer does not have an occupational pension scheme, they can elect to contribute to their employees' PRSAs. Tax relief for contributions, if relevant, are similar to that outlined in the above table for pensions. The growth in the value of the fund is tax-free. The fund can be realised when an individual is between 60 and 75 years old. Like other pensions it can be set up to provide a lump sum, an annuity or a combination of both.

TAX RELIEF ON PERSONAL PENSION CONTRIBUTIONS (UK)

As an incentive to promote personal pensions, the UK Government also allows tax relief on contributions made to personal pension schemes. Therefore, in the UK, pension contributions attract tax relief at the 20% tax band level and national insurance contributions relief at 8% (2008/09 rates)[10]. The maximum amount on which an individual can claim tax relief in any tax year is the greater of the individual's UK relevant earnings, up to a limit, and £3,600. In the tax year 2008/09, individuals can contribute up to £235,000 per year, from their relevant earnings into a pension fund and obtain tax relief[11]. Any contribution above this does not obtain tax relief. This limit does not apply in the year that full pension

[10] In 2007/08 relief was available at the 22% tax band level. The NIC for self-employed individuals is 8%.
[11] In 2007/08 the yearly limit was £225,000.

benefits are taken. ***Relevant earnings*** are emoluments that are chargeable to schedule E taxation (including benefits-in-kind) and profits from a trade, vocation or profession chargeable under schedule D.

In a personal pension scheme the individual pays the net amount and the government provides a tax credit to the pension provider worth 25% of the net amount paid to the pension company (this equates to 20% of the gross contribution). For example, where an individual has no relevant earnings, they can only contribute £3,600 to their pension fund. This is gross. In this instance they pay £2,880 (£3,600 x 80%) to the fund and the government pays £720 (£3,600 x 20%). Where the individual is a 40% taxpayer, they have to contact the revenue directly to claim the additional 20% relief available to them (The government only credits 20% to personal pension funds).

WORKED EXAMPLE 2 (The tax treatment of personal pension schemes)

B. Good is self-employed. He earned £15,000 last year. He is 62, is wealthy and has no liquidity problems.

Required
What is the maximum amount that B. Good can contribute to his personal pension scheme, relating to the income he earned last year?

Solution
B. Good can contribute a gross amount of £15,000 to his personal pension scheme. This means that he should pay a cheque to the pension scheme administrators of £12,000 (£15,000 × 80%). The government will then contribute £3,000, taking the total contribution up to £15,000 (his net relevant earnings).

Furthermore, there is a lifetime allowance on the value of a pension fund of £1.65 million (tax year 2008/09)[12]. Where the fund exceeds £1.65 million in value, the excess can be taken out as a lump sum – taxed at 55% (recovery charge), or the individual can withdraw the excess as income. This will be taxed at source at the rate of 25%. The remaining 75% that is paid to the pensioner is also subject to income tax. At present, an annual pension of about £80,000 is deemed to reflect a fund of about £1.65 million. Therefore, a pensioner will only receive 75% of any pension income paid above the £80,000 limit and will be taxed on that.

The following formula is sometimes used to determine if an individual's pension scheme value is above the lifetime allowance:

LTA% = Annual pension × 20 + (Lump sum/Lifetime allowance × 100)

The LTA% is the lifetime allowance percentage. If this equation works out at over 100% then the pension fund built-up will have exceeded the lifetime allowance percentage and a tax change will be payable on the excess.

FLEXIBLE PRIVATE PENSION (UK)

Stakeholder pensions are a form of personal pension. The difference between stakeholder pensions and other personal pensions is that they have to meet government standards. The requirements are that they should be flexible (have very low management charges and the ability to stop and start repayments) and have limited management charges. In all other respects they are the same as personal pensions.

OCCUPATIONAL/COMPANY PENSION SCHEMES

Company pension schemes are sometimes referred to as **occupational pension schemes**. When a company offers a company pension scheme, this usually means that they will contribute to the pension scheme on an individual's behalf, so long as the individual also contributes to the scheme.

---

[12] In 2007/08 the lifetime allowance fund limit was £1.6 million.

The tax treatment of company pension schemes is similar to that in a personal pension scheme except that the employer deducts the pension contribution from the individual's relevant earnings before determining their tax for the year. This is how the government provide their tax credit to the individual. Therefore, only the individual and their employer place funds in the scheme, not the government. The treatment is best explained using an example.

WORKED EXAMPLE 3   (Tax treatment of company pension schemes)

B. Good is employed. He earns €/£5,000 each month. He is a member of the company's pension scheme, in which employees pay 8% of their earnings and the employer pays 4%.

Required
a) Determine the monthly salary that will be subject to taxation.
b) Determine the monthly contribution to the pension scheme on behalf of B. Good.

Solution
a) B. Good will pay €/£300 (€/£5,000 x 8%) each month into the pension scheme. This means that B. Good will only be taxed on €/£4,700 (€/£5,000 − €/£300). Therefore, the tax relief is given at source.
b) The total contribution to the pension scheme each month on behalf of B. Good is €/£500 (€/£300 + (€/£5,000 × 4%)).

Tax relief in the ROI for company pension schemes

An individual who pays tax at the standard rate will be entitled to a tax refund of 26%[13] up to the limits outlined previously. A higher rate taxpayer will be entitled to relief at 43%[14].

Tax relief in the UK for company pension schemes

In the UK, pension contributions attract tax relief at the 20% tax band level and national insurance contributions relief at 11% (2008/09 rates)[15] if a lower rate taxpayer and at 41% (2008/09 rates) if a higher rate taxpayer[16].

TYPES OF COMPANY PENSION SCHEME

Company pension schemes are of two types: defined contribution and defined benefit schemes.

Defined benefit schemes

Defined benefit schemes are also referred to as **'salary related'** pension schemes. Defined benefit schemes are usually guaranteed, the pension amount being calculated is either a fraction or percentage of an employee's final salary, a fraction or percentage of their average salary over the final three to five years, or a fraction or percentage of the average salary of the employee over their full career. The latter is referred to as the **Career Average Re-valued Earnings (CARE) scheme**. The fraction is usually calculated with reference to the number of years and months of service given to the employer (i.e. number of years and months that the employee has contributed to the pension scheme divided by the maximum number of years as set by the pension scheme – this is commonly 80).

---

[13] PAYE relief at 20% plus PRSI relief at 6% (2008 rates)

[14] PAYE relief at 41% plus PRSI relief at 2% (2008 rates)

[15] In 2007/08 relief was available at the 22% PAYE tax band level.

[16] PAYE relief at 40% plus NIC relief at 1% (2008/09 rate)

WORKED EXAMPLE 4 (defined benefit schemes)

R. Hood has been working for the University of Ireland for the past 15 years and four months. He earns €/£60,000 per annum and has contributed to the pension fund since joining the university. The university's pension scheme is a final salary defined benefit scheme. It pays an annual pension related to the number of years and months that the employee contributed to the scheme, divided by 80. In addition to this, the scheme pays out a lump sum of three times the amount of the standard pension.

Required

a) Assuming that R. Hood's final salary is €/£60,000, calculate the annual pension he should expect to receive from the university's pension scheme.
b) Advise R. Hood of the amount of the lump sum that he should expect to receive.

Solution

a) R. Hood's annual pension can be calculated using the following formula:

$$\frac{\text{Years and days}/365}{80} \times \text{pensionable salary} = \text{Annual pension}$$

$$\frac{15 \text{ plus } 122/365}{80} \times €/£60{,}000 = €/£11{,}500$$

This equates to a monthly pension of €/£958 (€/£11,500/12). This is subject to income tax.

a) In addition R. Hood will receive a lump sum equal to:
€/£pension × 3 = €/£lump sum
€/£11,500 × 3 = €/£34,500

Defined benefit company pension schemes that are administered by companies have become unpopular over the past 20 years. From a company's perspective, defined benefit schemes have become too expensive. When the stock market fell in the 1990s so did the value of pension assets, and companies were left with large pension deficits that they were liable for.

The current accounting regulations insist that a company's pension liability be shown on the company's balance sheet. This is deemed to be unattractive to company directors. Then there is the actual annual cost, with some companies having to pay 20% of employee salaries into the company's pension scheme. There has also been the problem of security. This issue first came to the public's attention in 1991 with the Robert Maxwell scandal. After his death, it emerged that he had used £440 million of the pension fund to purchase shares in his own companies to boost their share price. This fraudulent behaviour affected 32,000 pensioners. Four years later the investment banks (including Goldman Sachs and Lehman Brothers) and the accountants (Coopers and Lybrand) agreed to fund part of the deficit, the government provided £100 million and the remaining Maxwell companies provided the rest in an out of court settlement (the total reimbursement was estimated at £376 million. This was still a loss to the pensioners as Robert Maxwell used £440 million that should have been invested to earn a return for the pensioners). A recent announcement by Gordon Brown's UK Government (December 2007) has indicated that the government will guarantee 90% of failed company pension schemes.

Defined contribution schemes

Defined contribution schemes (otherwise known as *money purchase schemes*) operate in a similar manner to personal pension schemes. A company contributes to the scheme on behalf of their employees, and pays this along with the employee's contribution to the pension fund administrator. The employee's contribution is deducted from their salary before the tax is calculated on their earnings. The contribution is normally a set percentage of an employee's salary, though most companies allow their employees to make *Additional*

Voluntary Contributions (AVCs). Like a private pension, the final pension will depend on the level of contributions made and the performance of the investment manager. When an employee leaves a company they usually cannot contribute to the scheme and become known as **deferred members**. In some instances the fund built up may be transferable to a new company scheme, or to a personal scheme. However, charges will be incurred if this happens.

Contracting out (UK)

In the UK, employed people can **opt out**, called **contracting out**, of the S2P. In this case the employer pays lower national insurance contributions to the government, and puts the balance into the company pension scheme instead (these individuals still qualify for the basic state pension, based on the lower national insurance contributions still being paid).

CONCLUSION

Pensions have historically been used to provide funds for individuals when they retire. There are two versions of pension: public pensions and private pensions. Public pensions are paid by the government from current national insurance contributions (UK)/social security contributions (ROI) to people who have contributed these taxes in the past. The level and type of public/state pension depends on the level of contributions made in the past. In the ROI individuals can either qualify for a contributory, or a non-contributory state pension. In the UK everyone who has paid the minimum level of national insurance contributions qualifies for the basic state pension, with people who contributed over the basic state level qualifying for a second state pension. In both cases a minimum level of income is guaranteed and an individual's income will be topped up to this level with a pension credit.

The other version of pension is private pensions. Private pensions involve the build up of a fund over an individual's life. This fund is then used to provide income for the retired individual. Pensions typically have three options, a lump sum (75% will be taxable), a monthly payment (an annuity) or a combination of both – 25% of the pension can be received in the form of a lump-sum, tax free. There are two types, personal pensions and occupational pensions. Individuals usually set-up and contribute to a personal pension when they do not have an occupational pension. Personal pensions are always contribution schemes (money-purchase schemes). Their final value is reliant on the performance of the fund. The individual bears all the risk. Most of the institutions who manage personal pensions invest heavily in the stock markets, so there is quite a bit of risk associated with the funds. Occupational pension schemes are set up by employers. Employees and the employer contribute to the pension. There are two types: defined contribution (money-purchase type scheme) and defined benefit (final salary). When the pension is a defined contribution scheme the individual bears all the risk (just like a personal pension scheme), when it is a defined benefit, the employer bears the risk, as they guarantee the pension. If the pension fund built-up is not large enough they have to make up the difference out of their reserves.

Regardless of the type of pension (public, personal or occupational) all pension income received by an individual is taxable (except the lump sum that can be paid when retirement starts).

Due to public demand, many pension schemes now offer ethical options, wherein they guarantee pensions that have not been built up by investment in what are deemed to be unethical businesses. These sorts of funds will not invest in companies that, for example, deal in arms, tobacco, alcohol, gambling, pornography, animal testing, exploitation of poor people and cause environmental damage.

Because of the poor performance of pension funds over the past two decades, confidence in pensions has decreased. Most individuals no longer rely solely on their pension for their retirement. Many individuals build up other investments, ISAs, properties, etc. for their retirement years.

KEY TERMS

Additional voluntary contributions

Basic state pension

Career average re-valued earnings schemes

Contracted out

Contributory state pension

Deferred members

Defined benefit scheme

Endowment policy

Final salary schemes

Lifetime allowance

Means tested

Money purchase pension schemes

National insurance contributions

Non-contributory state pension

Pay-as-you-go policy

Pay Related Social Insurance (PRSI)

Pension credit

Pension fund

Pensioners guaranteed income bonds

Personal Retirement Saving's Accounts (PRSA)

Relevant earnings

Stakeholder pensions

State earnings related pension scheme

State second pension

Transition state pension

WEBSITES THAT MAY BE OF USE

For more information on pensions in the UK visit the following site:

http://direct.gov.uk/en/MoneyTaxAndBenefits/Pensions AndRetirement/BeginnersGuideToPensions/DG_10026927

For information on pensions in the ROI visit the following site:
http://www.welfare.ie/

For information on personal finance and pensions in the ROI visit the following:
http://www.citizensinformation.ie/

REVIEW QUESTIONS

(Answers to review questions are provided in Appendix three)

1. What is a pension?
2. Explain the differences between a public and a private pension.

3. Explain the differences between a personal and an occupational pension scheme.
4. Explain the differences between a defined contribution and a defined benefit scheme.
5. How is pension income taxed on a retired individual?
6. Thomas earns €/£4,000 per month working for AIJ Ltd. He is a member of their occupational pension scheme. He contributes 10% per annum and the company contributes 3% per annum.

Required

a) Calculate the amount of Thomas' salary which will be subject to taxation.
b) Calculate the amount that will be paid into the pension scheme each month by AIJ Ltd.

7. Thomas has been working for AIJ Ltd. for the past 22 years and ten months. The pension is a final-salary defined benefit pension which pays an annual pension related to the number of years and months that the employee contributed to the scheme, divided by 80. In addition to this, the scheme pays out a lump-sum equal to three times the annual pension.

Required

a) Given the information in question six, calculate the expected monthly pension that Thomas should receive from the company's pension scheme.
b) What lump sum should Thomas expect to receive?

CHAPTER 10

REGULATION OF THE FINANCIAL SERVICES MARKETS

LEARNING OBJECTIVES

Upon completion of this chapter, readers should be able to:

- Explain the meaning of the key terms listed at the end of the chapter;
- Describe the regulation of financial services in the ROI/ UK; and
- Describe the steps to take when negligence is suspected.

REGULATION (ROI)

In the ROI the financial services industry is monitored by the *Irish Financial Services Regulatory Authority* (IFSRA).

The IFSRA

The IFSRA entity was established on 1 May 2003 to regulate all the financial service businesses in the ROI and to protect the customers of these firms. The IFRSA is part of the Central Bank and Financial Services Authority of Ireland, and is independent of the government. The IFSRA try to ensure that financial service businesses are sound, growing and solvent (this promotes confidence in the sector) and to assist financial service customers to make informed decisions about their financial affairs. Their focus in trying to protect consumers is more on problem prevention. The IFSRA provide information on the costs, risks and benefits of various financial products and services that are available in the ROI. They also monitor competition in the financial service sector and enforce rules on financial service firms who sell products to consumers, to ensure that the transactions are ethical and in customers' best interests.

Negligence suspected

Negligence occurs when a financial adviser does not exercise due care, or fails to do what is reasonable and prudent under the circumstances. When an individual feels that they were mislead by a financial adviser when being sold a financial services product, they can contact the IFSRA for advice on how to proceed. All financial services firms in the ROI have to comply with a Code of Conduct (i.e. to act in a fair and transparent manner). Steps to take when a customer is unhappy with the advice received (suspects negligence) are outlined in the following insert.

Steps to take when negligence is suspected:

1. *Initial contact:* Contact the firm who sold the product, explain the concerns and state clearly the required outcome.
2. *Formal complaint:* If the problem is not resolved, contact the firm in writing with a formal complaint. Include all details and specify the outcome required.
3. *Ombudsman:* When unhappy with the response received from the firm, contact the relevant **ombudsman** (an independent complaint scheme that is free of charge for consumers). They can recommend a solution, or pay out compensation. In the ROI there are two ombudsman services for financial products: the Financial Services Ombudsman and the Pensions Ombudsman.
4. *Courts:* When unhappy with the decision of the ombudsman an individual can appeal their decision in the High Court.

The *Financial Services Ombudsman (FSO)* is a free independent and impartial service which was established by the Central Bank and Financial Services Authority of Ireland Act (2004). It became operational on 1 April 2005. The FSO is a statutory officer who deals with complaints from consumers about their individual dealings with financial services providers, where the complaint has not been resolved by the provider. They deal with personal pensions, but complaints in respect of occupational pension schemes and PRSAs are dealt with by the pensions' ombudsman. The *pensions' ombudsman* is also a free, independent and impartial service. Complaints are restricted to instances where the consumer considers that they have suffered financial loss because the pension scheme or PRSA was not managed properly (administration issues).

The IFSRA also audit and monitor the practices of financial service firms and take punitive action if required. The most notorious recent investigations undertaken by the IFSRA involved the Allied Irish Bank and the National Irish Bank, when it found that these banks were overcharging customers.

REGULATION (UK)

Historically the financial services in the UK were self-regulated under the Financial Services Act (1986) and the Securities and Investments Board (SIB). However, there were many scandals in the mid-1990s which suggested that self-regulation was not protecting the public. The main issue was mis-selling. *Mis-selling* is where an advised sale does not meet the Financial Services Authority's (FSA) standards. Examples of mis-selling during the early to mid-1990s included: encouraging people to leave occupational pension schemes and join personal pensions; encouraging people to take out endowment mortgages without highlighting the risks; selling split-capital investment trusts as low-risk when they are not and encouraging individuals (particularly the elderly) to take out equity release mortgages when the individual was not made aware of the consequences. On investigation it became clear that the main perpetrators of mis-selling were the most influential entities under the self-regulatory system. Therefore, in 1997 an independent body was established to regulate the sector under the FSA. This system changed again in December 2001; the FSA itself received statutory powers under the Financial Services and Markets Act (2000) to regulate the financial services industry in the UK directly.

The Financial Services Authority

The *Financial Services Authority* (FSA) is an independent non-governmental body. It currently regulates the financial services industry in the UK. All firms that wish to undertake financial service activities have to be registered with the FSA. Indeed, it is a criminal offence to give advice without being authorised by the FSA. Financial advisers must demonstrate competence (hold a relevant qualification), honesty and be financially sound. If a financial adviser is called 'independent' they must advise across a range of providers (*depolarisation*). The FSA has three strategic aims:

* to promote efficient and orderly markets;
* to help financial service consumers achieve a fair deal; and
* to improve its own business capability and effectiveness.

To assist individuals, the FSA provides information on all the financial products that are available in the UK and will also provide advice/guidance when an individual considers that they have been treated negligently by a financial adviser.

Negligence suspected

Negligence occurs when a financial adviser does not exercise due care, or fails to do what is reasonable and prudent under the circumstances. The steps to take when negligence is suspected are similar to those outlined above for the ROI.

Steps to take when negligence is suspected:

1. *Initial contact:* Contact the firm who sold the product, explain the concerns and state clearly the required outcome.
2. *Formal complaint:* If the problem is not resolved, contact the firm in writing with a formal complaint. Include all details and specify the outcome required.
3. *Ombudsman:* When unhappy with the response received from the firm, contact the relevant ombudsman. They can recommend a solution, or pay out compensation.
4. *Courts:* When unhappy with the decision of the ombudsman an individual can appeal their decision in the High Court.

In the UK the Ombudsman is the **Financial Ombudsman Service** (FOS). The ombudsman will help solve disputes between customers and *regulated* firms. The FSA requires that all financial advisers have professional indemnity insurance. If an entity is found guilty of mis-selling then their professional indemnity insurance can be claimed against. The result is that in the future the yearly premium will increase. The entity may also have to pay a fine, court costs and/or compensation to the victims. In addition, the entity may loose their regulated status. If the offence is regarded as being fraudulent, the relevant financial advisers could even end up going to jail. When the professional indemnity insurance company does not investigate the claims of a customer, or does not meet a compensation claim, then the **Financial Services Compensation Scheme** (FSCS) can investigate and pay compensation (this is only available to those entities that are regulated by the FSA and may be limited).

The FSA also takes action against financial service firms that are not trading ethically. For example on 14 January 2008 the FSA fined 'Square Mile Securities' £250,000 for persistently using high pressure sales tactics and misleading information to sell customers (particularly elderly individuals) risky shares that they did not want/could not afford. On 17 January 2008 they fined the HFC Bank[1] over £1 million for not applying proper procedures when selling payment protection insurance. Many customers perceived that they required payment protection insurance, when they did not.

KEY TERMS

Depolarisation

Financial ombudsman
  service

Financial services authority

Financial services
  compensation scheme

Financial services
  ombudsman

Irish Financial Services
  Regulatory Authority
  (IFSRA)

Mis-selling

Negligence

Pensions ombudsman

---

[1] A HSBC holdings owned bank.

WEBSITES THAT MAY BE OF USE

For information on regulation of personal finance in the ROI visit the following site:
http://www.ifsra.ie/

For information on the role of the Financial Services Ombudsman (FSO) in the ROI visit:
http://www.financialservicesombudsman.ie/

For information on the role of the Pensions Ombudsman in the ROI visit:
http://www.pensions.ombudsman.ie/

For information on regulation of personal finance in the UK visit the following site:
http://www.fsa.gov.uk/

For more detail on the role of the FOS visit the following website:
http://www.financial-ombudsman.org.uk/

For more detail on the financial services compensation scheme available in the UK visit the following website:
http://www.fscs.org.uk/

REVIEW QUESTIONS

(Answers to review questions are provided in Appendix three)

1. What steps should an individual take when they suspect that they have been dealt with negligently by their financial adviser?
2. Outline the currently regulatory regime for financial services in your region (ROI/UK).

APPENDICES

APPENDIX 1

PRESENT VALUE DISCOUNT FACTOR TABLE

Present value of 1, ie $(1 + r)^{-n}$. Where r is the discount rate and n is the number of periods until payment.

Periods

(n)	1%	2%	3%	4%	5%	6%	7%	8%	9%	10%
1	0.990	0.980	0.971	0.962	0.952	0.943	0.935	0.926	0.917	0.909
2	0.980	0.961	0.943	0.925	0.907	0.890	0.873	0.857	0.842	0.826
3	0.971	0.942	0.915	0.889	0.864	0.840	0.816	0.794	0.772	0.751
4	0.961	0.924	0.888	0.855	0.823	0.792	0.763	0.735	0.708	0.683
5	0.951	0.906	0.863	0.822	0.784	0.747	0.713	0.681	0.650	0.621
6	0.942	0.888	0.837	0.790	0.746	0.705	0.666	0.630	0.596	0.564
7	0.933	0.871	0.813	0.760	0.711	0.665	0.623	0.583	0.547	0.513
8	0.923	0.853	0.789	0.731	0.677	0.627	0.582	0.540	0.502	0.467
9	0.914	0.837	0.766	0.703	0.645	0.592	0.544	0.500	0.460	0.424
10	0.905	0.820	0.744	0.676	0.614	0.558	0.508	0.463	0.422	0.386
11	0.896	0.804	0.722	0.650	0.585	0.527	0.475	0.429	0.388	0.350
12	0.887	0.788	0.701	0.625	0.557	0.497	0.444	0.397	0.356	0.319

Discount rates (r)

	11%	12%	13%	14%	15%	16%	17%	18%	19%	20%
13	0.879	0.773	0.681	0.601	0.530	0.469	0.415	0.368	0.326	0.290
14	0.870	0.758	0.661	0.577	0.505	0.442	0.388	0.340	0.299	0.263
15	0.861	0.743	0.642	0.555	0.481	0.417	0.362	0.315	0.275	0.239

	11%	12%	13%	14%	15%	16%	17%	18%	19%	20%
1	0.901	0.893	0.885	0.877	0.870	0.862	0.855	0.847	0.840	0.833
2	0.812	0.797	0.783	0.769	0.756	0.743	0.731	0.718	0.706	0.694
3	0.731	0.712	0.693	0.675	0.658	0.641	0.624	0.609	0.593	0.579
4	0.659	0.636	0.613	0.592	0.572	0.552	0.534	0.516	0.499	0.482
5	0.593	0.567	0.543	0.519	0.497	0.476	0.456	0.437	0.419	0.402
6	0.535	0.507	0.480	0.456	0.432	0.410	0.390	0.370	0.352	0.335
7	0.482	0.452	0.425	0.400	0.376	0.354	0.333	0.314	0.296	0.279
8	0.434	0.404	0.376	0.351	0.327	0.305	0.285	0.266	0.249	0.233
9	0.391	0.361	0.333	0.308	0.284	0.263	0.243	0.225	0.209	0.194
10	0.352	0.322	0.295	0.270	0.247	0.227	0.208	0.191	0.176	0.162
11	0.317	0.287	0.261	0.237	0.215	0.195	0.178	0.162	0.148	0.135
12	0.286	0.257	0.231	0.208	0.187	0.168	0.152	0.137	0.124	0.112
13	0.258	0.229	0.204	0.182	0.163	0.145	0.130	0.116	0.104	0.093
14	0.232	0.205	0.181	0.160	0.141	0.125	0.111	0.099	0.088	0.078
15	0.209	0.183	0.160	0.140	0.123	0.108	0.095	0.084	0.074	0.065

PRESENT VALUE DISCOUNT FACTOR TABLE (continued)

Discount rates (r)

Periods (n)	21%	22%	23%	24%	25%	26%	27%	28%	29%	30%
1	0.826	0.820	0.813	0.807	0.800	0.794	0.787	0.781	0.775	0.769
2	0.683	0.672	0.661	0.650	0.640	0.630	0.620	0.610	0.601	0.592
3	0.565	0.551	0.537	0.525	0.512	0.500	0.488	0.477	0.466	0.455
4	0.467	0.451	0.437	0.423	0.410	0.397	0.384	0.373	0.361	0.350
5	0.386	0.370	0.355	0.341	0.328	0.315	0.303	0.291	0.280	0.269
6	0.319	0.303	0.289	0.275	0.262	0.250	0.238	0.227	0.217	0.207
7	0.263	0.249	0.235	0.222	0.210	0.198	0.188	0.178	0.168	0.159
8	0.218	0.204	0.191	0.179	0.168	0.157	0.148	0.139	0.130	0.123
9	0.180	0.167	0.155	0.144	0.134	0.125	0.116	0.108	0.101	0.094
10	0.149	0.137	0.126	0.116	0.107	0.099	0.092	0.085	0.078	0.073
11	0.123	0.112	0.103	0.094	0.086	0.079	0.072	0.066	0.061	0.056
12	0.102	0.092	0.083	0.076	0.069	0.063	0.057	0.052	0.047	0.043
13	0.084	0.075	0.068	0.061	0.055	0.050	0.045	0.040	0.037	0.033
14	0.069	0.062	0.055	0.049	0.044	0.039	0.035	0.032	0.028	0.025
15	0.057	0.051	0.045	0.040	0.035	0.031	0.028	0.025	0.022	0.020

APPENDIX 2

ANNUITY FACTOR TABLE

Present value of an annuity of 1, ie $\dfrac{1-(1+r)^{-n}}{r}$ Where r is the discount rate and n is the number of periods.

Periods (n)	Discount rates (r)									
	1%	2%	3%	4%	5%	6%	7%	8%	9%	10%
1	0.990	0.980	0.971	0.962	0.952	0.943	0.935	0.926	0.917	0.909
2	1.970	1.942	1.913	1.886	1.859	1.833	1.808	1.783	1.759	1.736
3	2.941	2.884	2.829	2.775	2.723	2.673	2.624	2.577	2.531	2.487
4	3.902	3.808	3.717	3.630	3.546	3.465	3.387	3.312	3.240	3.170
5	4.853	4.713	4.580	4.452	4.329	4.212	4.100	3.993	3.890	3.791
6	5.795	5.601	5.417	5.242	5.076	4.917	4.767	4.623	4.486	4.355
7	6.728	6.472	6.230	6.002	5.786	5.582	5.389	5.206	5.033	4.868
8	7.652	7.325	7.020	6.733	6.463	6.210	5.971	5.747	5.535	5.335
9	8.566	8.162	7.786	7.435	7.108	6.802	6.515	6.247	5.995	5.759
10	9.471	8.983	8.530	8.111	7.722	7.360	7.024	6.710	6.418	6.145
11	10.368	9.787	9.253	8.760	8.306	7.887	7.499	7.139	6.805	6.495
12	11.255	10.575	9.954	9.385	8.863	8.384	7.943	7.536	7.161	6.814

Discount rates (r)

Periods (n)	1%	2%	3%	4%	5%	6%	7%	8%	9%	10%
13	12.134	11.348	10.635	9.986	9.394	8.853	8.358	7.904	7.487	7.103
14	13.004	12.106	11.296	10.563	9.899	9.295	8.745	8.244	7.786	7.367
15	13.865	12.849	11.938	11.118	10.380	9.712	9.108	8.559	8.061	7.606

Periods (n)	11%	12%	13%	14%	15%	16%	17%	18%	19%	20%
1	0.901	0.893	0.885	0.877	0.870	0.862	0.855	0.847	0.840	0.833
2	1.713	1.690	1.668	1.647	1.626	1.605	1.585	1.566	1.547	1.528
3	2.444	2.402	2.361	2.322	2.283	2.246	2.210	2.174	2.140	2.106
4	3.102	3.037	2.974	2.914	2.855	2.798	2.743	2.690	2.639	2.589
5	3.696	3.605	3.517	3.433	3.352	3.274	3.199	3.127	3.058	2.991
6	4.231	4.111	3.998	3.889	3.784	3.685	3.589	3.498	3.410	3.326
7	4.712	4.564	4.423	4.288	4.160	4.039	3.922	3.812	3.706	3.605
8	5.146	4.968	4.799	4.639	4.487	4.344	4.207	4.078	3.954	3.837
9	5.537	5.328	5.132	4.946	4.772	4.607	4.451	4.303	4.163	4.031
10	5.889	5.650	5.426	5.216	5.019	4.833	4.659	4.494	4.339	4.192
11	6.207	5.938	5.687	5.453	5.234	5.029	4.836	4.656	4.486	4.327
12	6.492	6.194	5.918	5.660	5.421	5.197	4.988	4.793	4.611	4.439

	21%	22%	23%	24%	25%	26%	27%	28%	29%	30%
13	6.750	6.424	6.122	5.842	5.583	5.342	5.118	4.910	4.715	4.533
14	6.982	6.628	6.302	6.002	5.724	5.468	5.229	5.008	4.802	4.611
15	7.191	6.811	6.462	6.142	5.847	5.575	5.324	5.092	4.876	4.675

	21%	**22%**	**23%**	**24%**	**25%**	**26%**	**27%**	**28%**	**29%**	**30%**
1	0.826	0.820	0.813	0.806	0.800	0.794	0.787	0.781	0.775	0.769
2	1.509	1.492	1.474	1.457	1.440	1.424	1.407	1.392	1.376	1.361
3	2.074	2.042	2.011	1.981	1.952	1.923	1.896	1.868	1.842	1.816
4	2.540	2.494	2.448	2.404	2.362	2.320	2.280	2.241	2.203	2.166
5	2.926	2.864	2.803	2.745	2.689	2.635	2.583	2.532	2.483	2.436
6	3.245	3.167	3.092	3.020	2.951	2.885	2.821	2.759	2.700	2.643
7	3.508	3.416	3.327	3.242	3.161	3.083	3.009	2.937	2.868	2.802
8	3.726	3.619	3.518	3.421	3.329	3.241	3.156	3.076	2.999	2.925
9	3.905	3.786	3.673	3.566	3.463	3.366	3.273	3.184	3.100	3.019
10	4.054	3.923	3.799	3.682	3.571	3.465	3.364	3.269	3.178	3.092
11	4.177	4.035	3.902	3.776	3.656	3.543	3.437	3.335	3.239	3.147
12	5.278	4.127	3.985	3.851	3.725	3.606	3.493	3.387	3.286	3.190
13	4.362	4.203	4.053	3.912	3.780	3.656	3.538	3.427	3.322	3.223
14	4.432	4.265	4.108	3.962	3.824	3.695	3.573	3.459	3.351	3.249
15	4.489	4.315	4.153	4.001	3.859	3.726	3.601	3.483	3.373	3.268

APPENDIX 3

SOLUTIONS TO REVIEW QUESTIONS

CHAPTER 2 SOLUTIONS

1. Though the government would like to provide for individuals' total welfare needs they are unable to do so. The following factors are examples of circumstances that have impacted on the government's ability to provide a welfare provision which provides financial security to individuals throughout their lives:

    *   People are living longer, hence pensions have become more costly.
    *   Birth rates are low – this means that fewer employees will be available to pay social security contributions and the government will be reliant on immigration to make up the deficit.
    *   Contributions to social security are dependent on the economy. In a boom economy, there are higher levels of contributions relative to when there is a recession.
    *   The population's demands are increasing all the time. What is regarded as a reasonable standard of living now would have been luxurious 50 years ago.
    *   Technological advances have meant that governments have to invest heavily in expensive equipment to provide the service demanded by the public (scanners, etc.).

The result is:

*   A move towards private health care, private dental care, private pensions and encouraging saving for retirement.
*   A change in the public pension which will mean it is less attractive in future years (particularly in the UK).
*   Higher social security contributions.

2. Most people have debt. When interest rates increase, the cost of debt increases and individuals' disposable incomes falls. This may impact on their quality of life and their ability to save, fund investments and make provision for their retirement. In the more extreme cases, where the individual has debt levels that are very high, financial distress may result. In the worst cases, where the individual can no longer meet the higher debt repayments, bankruptcy will occur.

3. The surge in oil prices has caused inflation to increase. Energy cost impacts on virtually every product that is bought or sold, as most are made with machines that either directly or indirectly are dependent on energy. Even goods that are not manufactured are impacted on – fruit and vegetables have to be transported, which requires oil. It may be that the increases in oil, will result in more domestic sourcing of perishable goods, etc. Inflation has the same impact as interest rate increases, it increases the amount that individuals have to spend each year, which reduces the amount of disposable income available for savings, investment and pension investments.

4. NI

   • ISAs.
   • Tax breaks for pension fund contributions.

   ROI

   • PRSAs.
   • SSIAs.
   • Tax breaks for pension fund contributions.

CHAPTER 3 SOLUTIONS

1. The key factors that should be considered in a financial plan include the following (as a minimum):

   Determine the net cash flows – identify areas where savings could be made if need be.

   Consider debt management – mortgage deal, credit card interest rates, loan rates, savings, set-off being used in the bank, etc.

Investments – what are they for, when are they expected to crystallise. If there are future commitments (i.e. education); consider investment options to suit the future needs.

Taxation – consider the influence of income tax, capital gains tax and inheritance tax on the current financial set-up and the impact on tax, of any advice given.

Consider risk – what are the current insurances; do they cover death (life cover), critical illness, unemployment (payment protection). Are income levels protected?

Retirement – the plan should refer to the wants of the individual when they retire, summarise the current steps taken and advise on whether there is a shortfall and the steps to take if there is.

Education planning – where there are children – determine the extent of support the individual is willing to give – assess the current steps taken to achieve this, highlight any shortfall and recommend action to alleviate the problem.

Care – determine if the individual has, or will have to care for themselves or for another party (disabled child, elderly parents, ageing self).

Succession – consider the steps taken to ensure wishes on death are known (will). Advise on the tax implications of the current will and suggest more tax efficient methods, if relevant.

2. Financial strategies to achieve financial independence might include the following: starting to budget and manage money; develop a savings plan; invest in equity shares or bonds; purchase property for investment purposes; invest in tax efficient savings products; invest in a pension.

3. Risk in personal financial planning is the chance that the individual's actual cash flows and life expectancy turn out to be different to what was predicted in the financial plan.

4. Statement of affairs for the businessman at the start of the period

Assets	€/£	Rate
Property		
Main family residence	400,000	
Investment property	150,000	
Credit union share account	3,000	4%
Deposit account	35,000	2.5%
ISA	15,000	5.5%
Current account	15,000	0.25%
Share portfolio	18,000	10%
	636,000	
Liabilities		
Mortgage	(180,000)	6.17% (see below)
Vehicle loan	(18,000)	26.82% (see below)
Credit card	(12,000)	12.68%
	(210,000)	
Net worth	426,000	

In addition, the businessman has a pension fund of €/£45,000 (this is untouchable until he is retired). Taking this into account his net worth is €/£471,000.

CHAPTER 4 SOLUTIONS

1. a) Students typically have little income. They should try to ensure that they leave college with the lowest level of debt that they can. Therefore, the focus of their financial plan should be on analysing expenditure and minimising debt. When analysing expenditure the focus is on reducing non-necessary expenditure and making the student aware of the amount they spend on various consumables. Whereas a budget for experiencing the 'student life' should not be ruled out, a limit should be placed on it.

Minimising the exposure to debt is very important. Student loans are available and these, apart from loans from family members, should be the first source of debt finance. Student loans typically charge inflation rates only, so will be the cheapest source of funds available. Students should be made aware of the pitfalls of using credit cards and other sources of bad debt.

b) Retired individuals will have two key areas that become more important than others, the first is structuring their investments, savings and pension funds in such a manner that they receive a suitable level of cash to maintain the lifestyle they planned for. This will involve making an estimate of life-expectancy.

The second is succession planning. A will should already have been created in earlier years, however, now is the time to update the will to include their wishes. It is recommended that individuals, who plan for success, make the heirs aware of their wishes. This is something that retired individuals might want to consider.

2. A 30 year-old person is likely to be employed, to have some savings, some debt, maybe own a house (with a mortgage) and a few assets. They are likely to have been paying into a pension scheme in their work and to have a reasonably high consumable spend. Given that the person is married, a premarital agreement is too late. The focus now should be on whether to integrate the couples' assets, or to keep them apart. If both parties own a property then the decision may have to be made to sell both and purchase one together, or to sell one, or rent one. Getting the documentation, deeds etc. changed to include both names is important if the decision is made to merge assets.

Other issues, less immediate, might include:

- Both parties should get together and revisit their financial plans, creating a new one between them.
- New objectives should be set.
- The couple should decide whether they are going to have children or not. The likely number of children, etc. should be considered.
- Estimates for the cost of this should be factored in, including whether they are going to pay for their children/s' education.
- Insurance will also have to be reviewed and the partner included on insurance policies.

- The pension company will need to be made aware of the spouse.
- Joint surplus funds can be determined and suitable investments reviewed.

3. The immediate issues to be dealt with are the redundancy money, the mortgage and the pension.

    If the redundancy money can cover the mortgage, and Percy has no other debt, then this would be one approach that could be taken. It would reduce Percy's financial risk in the future, as the fixed mortgage repayment would not need to be made.

    As Percy has worked for the same company for 20 years, he has probably built up quite a pension pot. He would need to get information on his options in relation to the pension. To remove pension funds before retirement is costly. The company seems strong – hence it might be better to leave the pension in the company until retirement (more detail would be requested).

    Pensions can no longer be relied on to provide for an individual when they retire, Percy will need to look at his assets (savings, other investments, etc. to see if they are sufficient to provide him with an income when he retires).

    Other factors need to be considered. Has Percy a partner who is earning? Is it likely that Percy will get another job? Are the company offering retraining? How is Percy's health? Etc.

    The financial plan will have to be completely changed to take account of the new cash flows, the risks reassessed and the objectives revisited.

4. The list might include information on the following:

    - Life insurance policies taken out by husband
    - Pension scheme paid into by husband (sometimes this will pay out on the death of the pension fund member)
    - Qualifications if any
    - View on working
    - Health
    - Debt
    - Savings
    - Mortgage (life insurance)

- House
- Investments
- Age of children
- Views on education of children
- Support for caring for children (parental support)
- Cash inflows expected from any source
- Benefits being received/possible financial help
- Views on downsizing property
- Number of vehicles in household (sell one?)

5. Most marketing people use affordability as a marketing ploy to entice people to purchase products/goods/services. People will think a product is good value if it can be obtained by paying out a small amount on a regular basis. If people have to pay one large bill, they would be a little more wary about spending money.

   The cash budget can be used to determine the actual spend on items, in yearly terms. It can make individuals more aware of the consequences of not keeping control of their money. Most people consider their income in yearly terms and even though they are well paid, cannot accumulate wealth, because they let the pounds/euro dribble away all year. For example, a coffee in Renoirs (a café beside the university I work in) is £1.70. Assume a person purchases one coffee every working week day (I nearly do) – this means that the person will spend £8.50 per week on coffee. In yearly terms (assume the person works 47 weeks of the year) this person spends £399.50 in cash, each year, just on coffee!!

   This sort of spending is no problem at all, so long as the person is on line with their finances to achieve their objectives (sufficient retirement fund, savings, paying debt, etc). However, if the person is living beyond their means, or is not going to achieve their financial objectives (for example, building up a deposit to purchase a house, or building up a good pension fund) then this budget can be used to highlight unnecessary expenditure. The person can then take steps to reduce their expenditure. For example, they could decide just to have coffee two days a week – saving £239.70 per year. Another option might be to decide that one phone will suffice, where an individual has both a landline and a mobile phone. They could decide that the satellite and cable channels are not worth it, etc. These are all luxury expenditures that should be curbed, when a person is living beyond their means.

Being frugal is recommended in a person's early financial life-cycle, as money has the greatest value to that category of person. When a person gets established, they naturally spend more, as the foundation blocks of their wealth have been created. When a person is being frugal they are more likely to build up a deposit for a house and also may be able to purchase a motor vehicle for cash. This immediately impacts on their net worth, as properties usually increase in value each year and the earlier an individual starts to pay off their mortgage, the quicker that property will be repaid before retirement. When an individual purchases a car using funds saved, not borrowed, they do not have monthly car repayments with interest to cover. This provides them with cash flexibility. Being frugal will also be interpreted in a positive light by the bank when an individual goes to obtain credit, even initial credit. Banks and other financial institutions consider people who have a strong savings record in a far better light. They are classed as being low risk and are likely to be able to negotiate a low rate for the debt they are seeking.

6. Comparison of financial goals and positions

Likely position:	Father	Son
Age	52	22
Income	High Surplus income	Low / Nil Income deficit
Dependants	Spouse Children Parents	None
Assets	Property Investments Pension	Nil
Liabilities	Debts (probably low)	Student loans

Likely goals:

Father

- Educate children.
- Low risk pension choices / planning for retirement (circa ten years to retirement).
- Reduce debt.
- Adequate insurance (Life, Health, Disability).
- Investments to be tailored with short / medium term access in mind and probably low risk given age profile.

Son

- Reduce debt.
- Full time earnings.
- Deposit for property purchase / rental.
- Car purchase.
- Holidays /Travel.
- Unlikely to have much interest/priority yet in pension / investments.

CHAPTER 5 SOLUTIONS

1. Insurance refers to policies that insure against the risk/chance/likelihood of something happening, like a nature disaster, or accidental death during the term of the policy.

    Assurance refers to policies that provide for something that is going to happen. The best example is death.

2. For some life assurance policies death does not have to occur through the term of the policy – **whole-of-life policies** – pay out on the death of the policy holder. These policies are more expensive than term assurance policies as the company providing the policy definitely has to payout on death. A policy which only pays out on death within the policy term is called a **term policy**. There are two types of whole-of-life policies. One involves the policy holder paying premiums for a set term after which the policy is treated as being paid up. The lump sum will be paid on death afterwards. The other option involves paying contributions for the rest of the policy holder's natural life. Whole-of-life policies might be used to cover expected inheritance tax liabilities on the individual's estate.

3. The most important insurance to a family man with three children is income protection both during his life (if he looses his job), or on his death. The policy should provide enough cover to keep the wife and children in their current lifestyle, at least until the children are educated and ready to leave home. By protecting current income, this should also be covering debt repayments, so the family's home should not be at risk because they are unable to pay their mortgage.

CHAPTER 6 SOLUTIONS

1. The annual percentage interest rate is: $(1 + 10\%/12)^{12} - 1)$ $= 10.47\%$

2. Any debt which is used to acquire an appreciating asset, or which improves overall financial health, is generally regarded as **'good debt'**. Whereas any debt which is used to finance items that depreciate in value, or are consumed, is considered **'bad debt'**. This type of debt will lead to an unhealthy financial position and may cause financial distress.

3.

a) The monthly interest rate is calculated as follows:
$(1 + r)^{12} - 1 = 24.8\%$
$1 + r = \sqrt[12]{1.248}$
$r = 1.863\%$ per month.

b) The current interest being charged per month is €/£5,000 × 1.863% = €/£93.15. As Fernando pays the minimum repayment amount of €/£300, this means that €/£206.85 (€/£300 − €/£93.15) must represent Fernando's monthly spend on consumables.

c) As a first step Fernando should use the €/£2,000 that he has built up in his current account to reduce this credit card debt. This is probably earning very little interest, but the bank manager would see it as a good financial move if it were used to reduce the expensive credit card debt.
   Fernando will be receiving an additional €/£500 cash inflow each month from now on. He should stop

spending on consumables using his credit card. If these expenditures are necessary he should now pay for them in cash. This will mean that €/£206.85 of his additional salary per month will be used to purchase consumables, leaving a balance of €/£293.15 for debt management. As Fernando does not wish to be left with any current liquidity issues (he may have no savings) it is recommended that only €/£250 of the surplus funds should be used to pay off the credit card each month. The remaining €/£43.15 should be accumulated in a savings account, as evidence to the bank manager that Fernando can save and is serious about improving his financial position. If his spending habits increase in line with his pay increase, this will send out a negative signal to the bank manager. Indeed, if Fernando is able to reduce his spending on consumables and to increase his savings per month this will provide an even stronger signal to the bank manager when he is assessing an application for a mortgage.

The new credit card monthly repayment will be €/£550 (the original €/£300 + the additional €/£250). The card will not be used to purchase anything again. Following this repayment schedule, Fernando should be able to repay this debt in six months.

Balance	Interest (1.863%)	Repayment	Closing balance
€/£5,000	€/£93.15	(€/£2,550)	€/£2,543.15
€/£2,543.15	€/£47.37	(€/£550)	€/£2,040.52
€/£2,040.52	€/£38.01	(€/£550)	€/£1,528.53
€/£1,528.53	€/£28.48	(€/£550)	€/£1,007.01
€/£1,007.01	€/£18.76	(€/£550)	€/£475.77
€/£475.77	€/£8.86	(€/£484.63)	-

(Cut up the card)

On viewing this, the bank manager will be able to see that Fernando is able to service debt at the rate of €/£550 per month. This will help him/her to determine how much Fernando will be able to afford to pay each month – which will influence the amount of debt the bank is willing to offer.

At this point, Fernando will also have amassed at least €/£258.90 (€/£43.15 × 6) in his bank account as well as any other monthly surpluses (that he used to have before) and in the six months following this, the balance should increase to a minimum of €/£3,817.80 (€/£258.90 + ((€43.15 + €/£550) × 12)).

4. The advantages of an IVA/FSA are as follows:

  (i) Not all creditors have to agree (60% will do for a FSA).
  (ii) All interest and charges are frozen.
  (iii) Once agreed to, the creditors cannot change their mind, they are legally bound by the agreement.
  (iv) Some of the debt will be written off.
  (v) It is based on affordability, not what you owe.
  (vi) An individual can manage their finances better as they just have to pay one monthly repayment, which is affordable and they know when the debt will be cleared.

5. Debt Management: Martin

a)

Debt schedule on: xx/xx/xxxx				
Debt source	**Interest rate**	**Balance**	**Minimum Repayment**	**Date due**
Mortgage	6.25%	€/£135,000	€/£1,200	1st
Car loan	10%	€/£6,000	€/£400	6th
Personal loan	13%	€/£10,000	€/£200	4th
Credit card A	^{1}18.15%	€/£4,000	€/£70	15th
Credit card B	^{2}23.14%	€/£5,500	€/£110	16th
Car insurance	^{3}26.85%	€/£1,000	€/£94.56	10th
Total		€/£161,500	€/£2,074.56	

Workings

1. The yearly rate of interest is:
    $((1 + 0.014)^{12} - 1) = 18.15\%$

2. The yearly rate of interest is:
    $((1 + 0.0175)^{12} - 1) = 23.14\%$

3. The rate of interest is:
    €/£95 × annuity for 12 periods = €/£1,000
    Annuity for 12 periods = €/£1,000/€/£94.56
    Annuity for 12 period = 10.575
    Which equates to 2% per period or $(1.02)^{12} - 1 =$ 26.82% per year.

b) The mortgage is the only debt that can be classed as 'good debt' as it is used to finance the purchase of a property. Properties usually appreciate in value. In all other instances the debt has been obtained to purchase items that depreciate in value or are consumables.

c) Martin currently has income of about €/£2,895 calculated as follows:

    The question tells us that Martin has received a pay rise of €/£500 per month and that this covers his debt repayments, cash expenditure and leaves him with €/£400 surplus. Therefore his salary must now be €/£2,895 (€/£2,075 as per the above debt schedule, an additional €/£320 which he is currently paying to the credit card companies ((€/250 × 2) − €/£70 − €/£110), €/£100 in additional cash expenditure and the €/£400 surplus).
    Before receiving the pay increase, Martin must have either used debt or his savings/current account to sustain his spending, as the €/£500 pay rise is only resulting in a €/£400 surplus when the debt and cash expenditure is covered!

Advice:
The advice given is limited to the information provided in the question and is limited to the terms of the question – which is advice on debt management.

As is identified in the 'debt schedule', the most expensive finance is the car insurance. Martin has a total of €/£3,000 between his savings and current account. It is good practice to retain an emergency balance, but it would make good economic sense to use €/£1,000 of the current account balance to pay for the insurance premium in one go and to put aside €/£80 each month to build up the balance again over the year. This would result in Martin having an additional €/£15 per month (based on the difference in his current monthly insurance spend €/£95 − €/£80), bringing his running cash surplus to €/£415 (€/£400 + €/£95 − €/£80) each month. As a priority he should focus on clearing his expensive debt, after this Martin should direct his attention to building up a suitable emergency savings reserve.

Martin has to stop using the credit cards. As the balances on the credit cards are not diminishing with the repayments, this means that Martin is purchasing €/£347.75 in goods each month using the cards (Card A: the repayment made is €/£250 − interest charged in each month of €/£56 (€/£4,000 × 1.4%) + Card B: repayment made €/£250 − interest charged in each month of €/£96.25 (€/£5,500 × 1.75%)).

This means that Martin is spending a total of €/£447.75 (€/£347.75 + €/£100 cash) each month on living expenses. The €/£347.75 is the difference between the current credit card repayments being made and the interest being charged by the credit card companies ((€/£250 − €/£56) + (€/£250 − €/£96.25)). These expenditures should be reviewed with a view to reducing the outflows, in the short term at least. Even if no efficiencies are notable, Martin could take some steps to improve his situation. Martin's focus should be on clearing the debt on credit card B as it incurs an annual interest rate of 23.14%.

To do this Martin should resort to paying the minimum balance on credit card A (which incurs an effective annual interest rate of 18.15%) and should redirect the balance of the repayments being made on this credit card to credit card B. This means that an additional €/£180 (€/£250 − €/£70) is now available to help clear the more expensive credit card B. The current minimum repayment on credit card A (€/£70) covers the interest cost that is payable (€/£5,000 × 1.4%) and it is assumed that Martin negotiates a deal with the credit card company to retain this minimum repayment amount for the next ten months.

Martin could continue to use credit card A for some monthly purchases so long as the limit on the card is not breached and there are no other hidden costs. This means that he can run up an additional €/£1,000 of debt on credit card A. This represents about three months of his current consumable expenses/credit purchases. Three months expenses amount to €/£1,043.25 (€/£347.75 × 3). This means that for three months Martin will be able to reduce the balance outstanding on credit card B by at least €/£845 (being the new €/£415 surplus cash plus the current repayment being made on credit card B (€/£250) – plus the cash that is available from not making the additional repayments of €/£180 on credit card A for the first three months.

Thereafter, the additional repayments will fall to €/£497.25 (€/£845.00 – €/£347.75) when Martin starts to use cash to pay for items that he was obtaining using credit card A and credit card B. At this point Martin will be paying for all his consumables in cash (€/£447.75).

Credit card B should be totally cleared within a ten-month period.

Credit Card B (Planned repayment schedule: version 1)

Balance	Interest (1.75%)	Repayment	Closing balance
€/£5,500	€/£96.25	(€/£845)	€/£4,751.25
€/£4,751.25	€/£83.15	(€/£845)	€/£3,989.40
€/£3,989.40	€/£69.81	(€/£845)	€/£3,214.21
€/£3,214.21	€/£56.25	(€/£497.25)	€/£2,773.21
€/£2,773.21	€/£48.53	(€/£497.25)	€/£2,324.49
€/£2,324.49	€/£40.68	(€/£497.25)	€/£1,867.92
€/£1,867.92	€/£32.69	(€/£497.25)	€/£1,403.36
€/£1,403.36	€/£24.56	(€/£497.25)	€/£930.67
€/£930.67	€/£16.29	(€/£497.25)	€/£449.71
€/£449.71	€/£7.87	(€/£457.58)	-

(Cut up the card)

If Martin were to use €/£1,000 from his current account immediately (leaving himself with €/£1,000 as an emergency reserve, which would be increasing by €/£80 per month as highlighted earlier), then he could repay this very expensive credit card off in eight months (see below). It is likely that the €/£1,000 being borrowed from Martin's emergency reserve could be repaid over the next one to two years – it may even be paid back sooner if savings can be made on cutting back on consumable expenditure (more detail is required). He also has the option of using the credit card again if required (though this should be avoided if at all possible).

Credit card B (Planned repayment schedule: version 2)

Balance	Interest (1.75%)	Repayment	Closing balance
€/£5,500	€/£96.25	(€/£1,845)	€/£3,751.25
€/£3,751.25	€/£65.65	(€/£845)	€/£2,971.90
€/£2,971.90	€/£52.00	(€/£845)	€/£2,178.90
€/£2,178.90	€/£38.13	(€/£497.25)	€/£1,719.78
€/£1,719.78	€/£30.09	(€/£497.25)	€/£1,252.62
€/£1,252.62	€/£21.92	(€/£497.25)	€/£777.29
€/£777.29	€/£13.60	(€/£497.25)	€/£293.64
€/£293.64	€/£5.14	(€/£298.78)	-

(Cut up the card)

After this period Martin should focus his attention on clearing credit card A. As mentioned previously, Martin will be paying for all his monthly consumables (€/£447.75) by cash. He will have monthly cash available before the payment on credit card A is taken into account of €/£1,015 (€500 + €/£15 + €/£250 + €/£250). He will firstly pay for his consumables in cash – €/£447.75, leaving a balance of €/£567.25, which can be used to pay credit card A.

Credit card A (Planned repayment schedule: version 1)

€/£5,000 = Annuity at 1.4% for Y periods × €/£567.25 (constant repayment amount)

€/£5,000/€/£567.25 = Annuity at 1.4% for Y periods.
8.81 = Annuity at 1.4% for Y periods.

This lies between 1% and 2% in the tables and an approximate timescale of between 9 and 10 months is predicted. After which time the card should be used occasionally, and the balance repaid monthly, before interest charges accrue.

The next debt item to clear is the personal loan. Before advice is provided on the personal loan and the motor vehicle, a copy of the loan agreement should be reviewed to determine if penalties are payable for early settlement, or for changing the repayment terms. If the repayment terms of either can be altered at no cost, then these loans could be reorganised to ensure that larger repayments are directed to the personal loan, which incurs a higher rate of interest, relative to the car loan. The current commitment in terms of the number of repayments left can be calculated as follows:

Personal loan

With an implicit interest rate of 13% the personal loan will be repaid in about 70 months, calculated as follows:

Monthly interest rate is:
$(1 + r)^{12} - 1 = 13\%$
$(1 + r)^{12} = 1.13$
$1 + r = \sqrt[12]{1.13}$
$r = 1.01\%$ per month

To find out the time left:
€/£200 × 1.01% annuity for Y periods = €/£10,000
1.01% annuity for Y periods = €/£10,000/€/£200
1.01% annuity for Y periods = 50

If there were no interest charges this loan would be repaid in 50 periods, so the remaining life must be greater than this.

The annuity formula is calculated using 70 time periods at a rate of 1.01% (this rate was selected by trial and error).

$$\text{Annuity factor formula} = \frac{1 - (1 + r)^{-n}}{r}$$

$$\text{Annuity factor} = \frac{1 - (1 + 0.0101)^{-70}}{0.0101}$$

$$= 50.01$$

Therefore under the current repayment schedule this loan will be repaid within 70 months (five years and ten months). By the time Martin will have cleared his credit cards, 21 months will have lapsed and 49 repayments instalments on this loan will still have to be covered.

Car loan

With an implicit interest rate of 10% the car loan will be repaid in about 16 months, calculated as follows:

Monthly interest rate is:
$(1 + r)^{12} - 1 = 10\%$
$(1 + r)^{12} = 1.1$
$1 + r = {}^{12}\sqrt{1.1}$
$r = 0.797\%$ (rounded to 0.8%)

To find out the time left:
€/£400 × 0.8% annuity for Y periods = €/£6,000
0.8% annuity for Y periods = €/£6,000/€/£400
0.8% annuity for Y periods = 15

By looking at the annuity tables for the closest rate (1%) an annuity factor value of 15 comes in between 16 and 17 periods. Trial and error is used to determine the closest time period. As 0.8% is lower than 1% the first attempt tries 15 periods.

The annuity formula is calculated using 15 time periods at a rate of 0.8% (n = 15, r = 0.008).

$$\text{Annuity factor formula} = \frac{1 - (1 + r)^{-n}}{r}$$

$$\text{Annuity factor} = \frac{1 - (1 + 8.008)^{-15}}{0.008}$$

$$= 14.08$$

The annuity formula is calculated using 16 time periods at a rate of 0.8%

$$\text{Annuity factor} = \frac{1 - (1 + 0.008)^{-16}}{0.008}$$

$$= 14.96$$

Therefore under the current repayment schedule this loan will be repaid within 16 months (n=16). This loan will be cleared before the second credit card is cleared. Therefore, in 16 months time, Martin may be able to speed up the repayment of credit card A by even more than the repayment amount specified above. This will result in clearing this credit card balance within nine periods. Martin will therefore be in stronger financial position in a total of 19 months time (ten months to clear credit card B, nine for credit card A). The repayments and balance on credit card A would now be as follows:

Credit Card A (Planned repayment schedule: version 2)

Balance	Interest (1.4%)	Repayment	Closing balance
€/£5,000	€/£70.00	(€/£567.25)	€/£4,502.75
€/£4,502.75	€/£63.04	(€/£567.25)	€/£3,998.54
€/£3,998.54	€/£55.98	(€/£567.25)	€/£3,487.27
€/£3,487.27	€/£48.82	(€/£567.25)	€/£2,968.84
€/£2,968.84	€/£41.56	(€/£567.25)	€/£2,443.15
€/£2,443.15	€/£34.20	(€/£567.25)	€/£1,910.10
€/£1,910.10	€/£26.74	(€/£967.25)*	€/£969.59
€/£969.59	€/£13.57	(€/£967.25)	€/£15.91
€/£15.91	€/£0.22	(€/£16.13)	-

(Cut up the card)

*(€/£567.25 + €/£400.00) where the additional €/£400 is available as the car loan is finished. These repayments would start 11 months from now and be completed by 19 months time.

If Martin takes the advice provided above onboard, he should be in a healthier financial position in two year's time. He will have cleared both credit cards, the car loan will be finished and it might be worthwhile at that stage reviewing the personal loan with a view to shortening the term of the loan and clearing the balance.

(It is recommended that Martin does not replace his car before the next review, as his savings are low, and we do not know if he is putting any funds aside for his retirement).

The mortgage is at a competitive rate, though a more competitive rate might be capable of negotiation if Martin is not tied into any deal that has a specific time limit. More information is required on the mortgage details.

CHAPTER 7 SOLUTIONS

1. Transactions motive – refers to the holding of cash to cover day-to-day operating expenditure, such as buying petrol for the car, groceries for the house, clothes, etc.

Precautionary motive - refers to the holding of a cash buffer to cover emergencies. It is sometimes referred to as an emergency fund. Unexpected emergencies may include the car breaking down, or losing your job. The level of funds held for precautionary motives depends on the risks associated with an individual's income. For example, an individual who has a secure job and is in good health with a new car can afford to hold less cash for precautionary motives.

Speculative motive - refers to the holding of cash to make money on opportunities that may arise, such as buying goods in bulk to achieve a cheaper price, paying for insurance up-front to reduce interest charges on any finance that is offered for spreading the payments over the period, or paying for goods up-front in cash to avail of a discount.

2. A current account deals with all the daily transactions affecting an individual. It normally has a cheque book and a debit card/bank card facility. In addition, several standing orders, or direct debits can be set up for a fee. Wages are normally paid into a current account and expenses, credit card instalments and loan repayments are paid out of it.

A deposit account is more like a savings account. Some offer instant access. This means that they may have a bank card which allows the account holder to withdraw funds from an automated teller machine (ATM). Instant access accounts can also be set up to receive regular direct debit transfers from the current account. Transfers in can also be set up and instigated using internet banking. They do not have a cheque book, or a debit card and the interest received is usually higher to that received on a current account. Term deposit accounts are more restrictive. Money is lodged and cannot be touched for the term agreed. Though inflexible, this type of account normally provides a higher rate of return.

3. ROI

  - Some AnPost savings accounts
  - Credit union dividends up to a limit of €635 per year
  - All savings products for individual who are over 65 years of age

  UK

  - Dividends received on credit union share accounts
  - ISAs
  - Premium bonds
  - Index linked savings certificates
  - Fixed interest savings certificates
  - Children's bonus bonds.

4. Personal financial plan

a) Statement of affairs for the businessman at the start of the period

Assets	€/£	Rate
Property		
Main family residence	400,000	
Investment property	150,000	
Credit union share account	3,000	4%
Deposit account	35,000	2.5%
ISA	15,000	5.5%
Current account	15,000	0.25%
Share portfolio	18,000	10%
	636,000	
Liabilities		
Mortgage	(180,000)	6.17% (see below)
Vehicle loan	(18,000)	26.82% (see below)
Credit card	(12,000)	12.68%
	(210,000)	
Net worth	426,000	

In addition, the businessman has a pension fund of €/£45,000 (this is untouchable until he is retired). Taking this into account his net worth is €/£471,000.

b)

Expected debt schedule for the year ended xx/xx/xx (including the insurances)				
Debt source	Interest rate	Balance	Minimum repayment	Date due
VISA payments	12.68%	€/£12,000	€/£1,200	Monthly
Vehicle loan	26.82%	€/£18,000	€/£1,400	Monthly
Life insurance	42.57%	€/£800	€/£80	Monthly
Permanent life insurance	26.82%	€/£750	€/£70	Monthly
Voluntary health insurance	10.00%	€/£500	€/£43.75	Monthly
Mortgage protection insurance	0%	€/£450	€/£37.50	Monthly
Loan protection insurance	42.57%	€/£300	€/£30	Monthly
Mortgage	6.17%	€/£180,000	€/£900	Monthly
Total		€£212,800	€/£3,761.25	

Cost and evaluation of current financing

Car finance
Repayments = €/£1,400 per month for 15 months

€/£1,400 × 15 =	21,000	(Total payments made)
Car cost	18,000	
Finance amount	3,000	

So €/£1,400 × annuity for 15 periods = €/£18,000
Annuity for 15 periods = €/£18,000/€/£1,400
Annuity for 15 periods = 12.85
Rate per the tables = 2% per month

Therefore, the yearly annual equivalent percentage is 26.82% $((1.02)^{12} - 1)$.

VISA
1% per month – in yearly terms $= (1.01)^{12} - 1 = 12.68\%$.

Life and sickness insurance
Life insurance

€/£80 × 12 =   960 (Total payments made to
                                         the insurance company)

Premium   800
Finance amount   160

Cost of finance $=$ €/£80 × 12 period annuity $=$ €/£800
12 period annuity $=$ €/£800/€/£80
12 period annuity $=$ 10
Rate per the tables $=$ 3% per month (rounded)
Therefore, the yearly annual equivalent percentage is 42.57%
       $((1.03)^{12} - 1)$.

Permanent life insurance

€/£70 × 12 =   840 (Total payments made to
                                         the insurance company)

Premium   750
Finance amount   90

Cost of finance $=$ €/£70 × 12 period annuity $=$ €/£750
12 period annuity $=$ €/£750/€/£70
12 period annuity $=$ 10.71
Rate per the tables $=$ 2% per month (rounded)
Therefore, the yearly annual equivalent percentage is 26.82%
       $((1.02)^{12} - 1)$.

Voluntary health insurance

€/£43.75 × 12 =   525 (Total payments made to
                                         the insurance company)

Premium   500
Finance amount   25

Cost of finance $=$ €/£43.75 × 12 period annuity $=$ €/£500
12 period annuity $=$ €/£500/€/£43.75
12 period annuity $=$ 11.42

By looking at the tables, it is clear that the monthly rate of interest is less than 1%; therefore, 0.8% is selected, to determine if it will result in an annuity factor score of 11.42, or close to this.

$$\text{Annuity factor formula} = \frac{1 - (1 + r)^{-n}}{r}$$

$$\text{Annuity factor} = \frac{1 - (1 + 0.008)^{-12}}{0.008}$$

$$= 11.39$$

Rate = 0.8% per month (rounded)
Therefore, the yearly annual equivalent percentage is 10.00% $((1.008)^{12} - 1)$.

Loan protection insurance

€/£30 × 12 =	360 (Total payments made to the insurance company)
Premium	300
Finance cost	60

Cost of finance = €/£30 × 12 period annuity = €/£300
12 period annuity = €/£300/€/£30
12 period annuity = 10.00
Rate per the tables = 3% per month (rounded)
Therefore, the yearly annual equivalent percentage is 42.57% $((1.03)^{12} - 1)$.

Mortgage
Yearly interest = €/£10,800/€/£180,000 = 6%
Permonth actual percentage is 0.5% (6%/12) or €/£900/€/£180,000.
Therefore, the yearly annual equivalent percentage is 6.17% $((1.005)^{12} - 1)$.

c) **Cash budget for the businessman for the year
   ended xx/xx/xx**

		€/£	
Earned income			
Self-employed			
business	(€/£3,500 × 12)	42,000	
Investment income			
Credit union dividend	(€/£3,000 × 4%)	120	
Bank deposit income	(€/£35,000 × 2.5% × 0.8)	700	
ISA	(€/£15,000 × 5.5%)	825	
Portfolio	(Dividends less tax)		
	€/£18,000 × 10% × 0.8	1,440	
		45,085	
Expected outflows			
VISA payments	(€/£1,200 × 12)	(14,400)	12.68%
Vehicle loan	(€/£1,400 × 12)	(16,800)	26.82%
Life insurance	(€/£80 × 12)	(960)	42.57%
Permanent life			
insurance	(€/£70 × 12)	(840)	26.82%
Voluntary health			
insurance	(€/£43.75 × 12)	(525)	10.00%
Mortgage protection			
insurance	(€/£37.50 × 12)	(450)	0%
Loan protection			
insurance	(€/£30 3 × 12)	(360)	42.57%
Mortgage	(€/£900 3 × 12)	(10,800)	6.17%
Pension	(€/£500 3 × 12)	(6,000)	
		(51,135)	

Net deficit in cash requirement   **(6,050)**

*(Students might also allow for additional tax of up to
€/£600 on the additional income, where they assume the
businessman is a higher rate tax-payer who will have to
pay tax at the higher tax level.)*

5. Personal financial plan – advice

a) **Cost and evaluation of current financing
    Car finance**
    Discount saving = €/£1,000/€/£18,000 = 5.55% for 15
    months
        (Can equate the interest rate to a yearly rate by sim-
    ply dividing the 5.55 by 15 and multiplying by 12)
    5.55% × 12/15 = 4.44%
        This should be compared to the cost of the financing
    (see solution 4 - 26.82%)

At present this is a very expensive form of finance.

This option should not have been taken and should be rescinded during the cooling off period in the contract. The businessman has €/£35,000 in a deposit account earning only 2.5% which is subject to tax (hence this equates to a return of about (2.5% (0.8) = 2% assuming a tax rate of 20%) which is just equal to inflation (indeed, the businessman is most probably going to have to pay tax at the higher rate band, hence will actually be earning a yearly return of below inflation rate). The €/£19,000 car should be paid for from this source of finance. There is a good chance of negotiating a cheaper price for a cash purchase. Shop around – try other dealers, consider importing.

VISA

Current cost (see solution 4) 12.68%

Compared to other VISA companies, this rate is not as bad as is sometimes charged. However, the rate far exceeds the interest that is being earned on the current account (normally less than 1%). I would advise paying off the VISA bill in full using the current account. This will leave a balance of €/£3,000 (€/£15,000 − €/£12,000). I am not saying that the businessman should stop using his VISA altogether, but he should start paying off the full balance each month, as he has the funds available to do so. Therefore, his monthly Visa payment will increase to about €/£1,500 per month (varying with spend).

Life and sickness insurance

Cost of life insurance is 42.57% (see solution 4)

Cost of permanent life insurance is 26.82% (see solution 4)

Cost of voluntary health insurance is 10.00% (see solution 4)

General

It would seem that the businessman is over-insured. I would recommend that the insurances be analysed to determine if there is a benefit to having all three. Though

I would need more information before a final decision is taken, it would seem that one of these could be cancelled, saving the businessman either €/£960 or €/£840 per year.

These insurances should be paid in cash. The rates of interest being charged for spreading the payment across the year are too high – ranging from 42.57% to 10.00%. There is sufficient cash in the current account to pay for these straight away.

I do not know your health profile. This is something we need to discuss to determine if the voluntary health insurance is required, and it may be that it also overlaps with one of the other two life and illness covers. This may potentially save €/£525 per year.

The cost of **loan protection insurance** is 42.57% (see question 2).

You pay two payment protection insurances costing you €/£360 + €/£450 per year = €/£810.

Before advising you further I would need to know if you have any dependents or a spouse. In addition, many payment protection insurances do not cover self-employed people – check this with the lending company – it might be that you are not covered in the event of you being unable to work. These policies are usually set up for people who are employed. At present, there are many cases where bank customers are reclaiming these payments from the bank, as they have been mis-sold to them. The FSA has recently penalised the HFC bank for selling this *type of insurance product to people who are not entitled to cover.*

With a mandate from yourself I could look into this for you. If the policies do cover you, it is a personal decision as to whether you keep them or not. I would point out that they are not necessary as you have quite a strong capital base. Liquidity is your main problem at the minute and I would definitely recommend that you do not pay payment protection on the vehicle loan (as mentioned earlier it is advisable to cancel this loan agreement and to pay for the car in cash anyway). This would save you €/£360 in the year. If you opt to retain the mortgage protection then I advise you to continue with the 12 monthly payments as you are not being charged any interest for financing this arrangement.

Mortgage

The yearly cost is 6.17% (see question 2).

Relative to the other forms of finance, this is your cheapest form of debt. I have a couple of suggestions. The debt is fixed to your home, and as such, you cannot claim a deduction for tax for the interest that is payable each year.

I would need to see the history of the mortgage to determine if the funds were used to purchase your main residence, or the investment property.

If at some stage you arranged the mortgage to purchase the investment property, then I recommend rearranging the debt so that it is encumbered to the investment property. You will be able to obtain a tax deduction for the interest charge each year, against any rental income received on that property (if you elect to rent it).

To hedge the businessman's income, the property should be renovated for the €/£10,000. Given that the property could be rented for €/£500 per month, the investment would pay for itself within one year and eight months (assuming the tenant pays utility bills). €/£500 × 12 = €/£6,000 per year. ((€/£4,000/€/£6,000) × 12) = 8 months. The deposit account funds could be used to finance this initial investment.

Other issues to consider – information required

A breakdown of the monthly expenditure (€/£1,500) should be requested. An analysis of this might highlight potential savings that can be made. The extent of VISA interest and charges should be checked.

What age is the businessman? This would help to determine if the pension asset was sufficient to cater for his retirement.

Should the businessman consider paying off some of the mortgage debt – though the rate is competitive 6.17% – the interest repayment is quite large and might be burdensome if the businessman's main source of income takes a downturn.

Summary of key advice points

The businessman is spending more than he is making – leading to a drain on his liquidity. Though he has plenty of liquid funds, these are not earning sufficient returns. The current account earns less than 1% per annum (below the inflation rate of 2% per annum), the deposit account earns 2.5% per annum (2% after tax) – so there is no real return. €/£50,000 is tied up in these accounts. The VISA account should be settled using the current account. The insurances that have not been cancelled should be paid in full (without the finance option – the exception being the mortgage protection insurance – if kept). These should be paid from the current account. (€/£15,000 – €/£12,000 – €/£800 – €/£500 leaving a balance of about €/£1,700).

The businessman is advised to purchase the car in cash using the deposit account. There is a cooling-off period in the contract. This means the contract can be broken without penalties being incurred. In addition, the properties are earning a strong capital return, but the investment property should be rented. Therefore, the €/£10,000 should be invested in making the property fit for renting. Funds from the deposit account should be used to finance this refurbishment. Finally, a small float should be maintained in the deposit account, with any remaining balance (€/£35,000 – €/£18,000 (car) - €/£10,000 (refurbishment) – €/£2,000 (float) = €/£5,000) being used to top up the tax-free ISA (in the UK – only €/£3,000[1] will be invested), widen the portfolio of shares (earns 10%), or to pay off some of the mortgage (this will be influenced by the age and risk profile of the individual). In this example I am assuming the latter option is taken and €/£2,000 will go against the mortgage when it is being renegotiated (in ROI the advice would be to pay the full €/£5,000 off the mortgage or pay it into the PRSA account). The businessman will still have a float (€/£1,700 will remain in the current account after the insurances are paid (€/£3,000 – €/£1,300) and

---

[1] In 2008 the maximum sum allowed to be deposited to an ISA increased to £3,600

€/£2,000 will remain in the deposit account to cover any short-term emergencies.

When re-mortgaging his home the businessman could allocate some of the debt to the rental property under a different mortgage. This will help to reduce/eliminate the tax bill on the property.

Given the strong cash inflows in the year it might be advisable for the individual to put the €/£3,000 that is in the credit union account against his mortgage, as he can build up this balance fairly quickly afterwards from his excess monthly cash. The security of his income in the future would influence this decision.

d) **New statement of affairs at the start of the year (assuming advice is taken)**

Assets	€/£	*Change recommended*	€/£
Property			
Main family residence	400,000	-	400,000
Investment property	150,000	10,000	160,000
Credit union account	3,000	(3,000)	-
Deposit account	35,000	(33,000)	2,000
ISA (PRSA account if ROI student)	15,000	3,000	18,000
Current account	15,000	(12,000)	3,000
Share portfolio	18,000	-	18,000
	636,000	(35,000)	601,000
Liabilities			
Mortgage – residential property	(180,000)	105,000	(75,000)
Mortgage – rental property	-	(100,000)	(100,000)
Vehicle loan	(18,000)	18,000	-
Credit card	(12,000)	12,000	-
	(210,000)	35,000	(175,000)
Net worth	426,000		426,000

It is expected that students from the ROI would not typically top up the ISA/Term deposit account. They should recognise the strong cash earnings potential of this individual and direct the funds from the term deposit into either repaying the mortgage, paying the funds into the PRSA account or purchasing shares in the portfolio (the advice will depend on the assumed profile of the businessman.)

b)

Estimated cash budget for the businessman for the forthcoming year (ended xx/xx/xx) Assuming the position is as per part (a) – variations will occur depending on the advice given and reflected in part (a).

		€/£
Earned income		
Self-employed business	(€/£3,500 × 12)	42,000
Investment income		
Rent	(€/£500 × 12)	6,000
Credit union dividend		-
Bank deposit income	(€/£2,000 × 2.5% × 0.8)	40
ISA/PRSA	(€/£18,000 × 5.5%)	990
Portfolio	(Dividends less tax)	
	€/£18,000 × 10% × 0.8	1,440
		50,470
Expected outflows		
VISA payments	(€/£1,500 × 12)	(18,000)
Vehicle loan	Cancelled	-
Life insurance		(800)
Permanent life insurance	Cancelled	-
Voluntary health insurance	Cancelled (?)	(500)
Mortgage protection insurance	(€/£37.50 × 12) Cancel?	(450)
Loan protection insurance	Cancelled	
Total mortgage interest*	(€/£875 × 12)	(10,500)
Pension	(€/£500 × 12)	(6,000)
		(36,250)
Net surplus in cash requirement		14,220

*(€/£175,000 × 0.5%) – It is assumed that the business-man will be able to retain the same rate that he currently repays, when he re-negotiates the mortgage.

If the car loan is paid off immediately and the above surplus results, then this surplus should be used to increase the emergency reserves in the savings accounts. In future years it could be invested in the share portfolio – earning another 10% per year (taxed at 10% at source) – £14,220 × 10% × 90% = €/£1,279.80 income.

If interest rates are set to rise, or the stock market is bearish, it might be better to pay the mortgage off with this surplus, but if the 10% return can be maintained, this would be the preferred choice of investment.

(Variations from this solution can result where students give different advice)

CHAPTER 8 SOLUTIONS

1. Bonds are traded debt. When a company or the govern-ment wishes to borrow funds, they can issue bonds. What they are selling is the promise to pay the holder of the bond a fixed amount of interest, called a coupon periodically (every six months or every year) and a set payment (usually €/£100) to redeem (repurchase) the bond at a set date in the future. These streams of future cash flows are bought and sold in the bond markets. The interest is guaranteed (so long as the company does not go into liquidation) and the redemption amount is also guaranteed. Indeed, a company must pay what they owe in bond interest before they can pay a dividend, so from an investor's viewpoint they are less risky than equity.

   Equity shares are different. The holder of an equity share might get a dividend and can sell the share. It is not redeemed, as such. When an individual purchases an equity share they become an owner of a portion (a share) of the company. Though the holder of the share is an owner and is entitled to vote at shareholder meetings, their power is restricted in respect of dividend distri-butions. Directors decide what dividend to pay. Share-holders can only reduce this at a shareholder meeting, they cannot increase it. Directors may decide not to pay a dividend at all and they must honour the bond interest before they pay any dividend. The value of an equity share typically moves with the value of the company, when the company performs poorly, or the economy has a turndown the value of equity usually falls, when the economy does well and the company is successful, the value of equity increases (share price increases). When the company performs poorly the directors may not pay any dividend, however, when it does well the level of dividend can be very high.

2. A risk-free investment is an investment that is virtually free from risk, such as gilts. It is very unlikely that the government will not be able to honour the coupon and redemption values.

3. The periodic payment can be calculated using the following formula:

$$P = \frac{M \times r}{1 - (1/(1+r)^t)}$$

Where P is the periodic payment (to find)
M is the initial size of the mortgage (€/£280,000)
t is the number of payments 180 (15 × 12)
r, the periodic interest rate, is 0.4167% (5%/12)

Therefore

$$P = \frac{€/£280{,}000 \times 0.004167}{1 - (1/(1+0.004167)^{180})}$$

$$P = €/£2{,}214.28$$

4. a) The interest payment each year to the bank will be €/£1,166.67 ((€/£280,000 × 5%)/12).
    The periodic payment to the endowment can be calculated using the following formula:

$$M = \frac{p((1+y)^t - 1)}{y}$$

Where
M, the target maturity amount, is €/£280,000
p is the periodic payment
t, the number of periods, is 15
and y, the rate of return expected to be earned by the fund, is 7%.

$$€/£280,000 = \frac{p((1+0.07)^{15} - 1)}{0.07}$$

$$€/£280,000 = p \times 25.129$$

$$€/£280,000/25.129 = p$$

$$€/£11,142.50 = p$$

Therefore the monthly payment to the endowment policy will be €/£928.54 (€/£11,142.50/12).
The total monthly payment will be €/£2,096.21 (€/£1,167.67 + €/£928.54)

b) When the calculations from question three and part a) above are compared it would seem that Geoffrey would be better off going for the endowment mortgage. He stands to gain €/£118.07 every month as the payment required is lower (€/£2,214.28 − €/£2,096.21). This money could be invested monthly and would accumulate to a good amount by the end of 15 years.

However, there are risks associated with endowment plans. They typically invest funds in the stock market and therefore are exposed to risk. In addition the management fees and transaction fees have to be covered. To estimate a return (net of all these costs) of 7% might be deemed to be unrealistic. Over the past 20 years endowment mortgages have been receiving bad press as many of them did not mature at the value expected. The return earned had been over-estimated in most instances. Though rare, endowments could outperform their initial predictions.

The option to take-up will depend on Geoffrey's attitude to risk and his views on how the equity markets will perform over the next fifteen years. If he feels that they will perform strongly, and he wants to take the chance, then this product is fine for him.

Geoffrey's views on interest rates will also impact on his choice. If an endowment mortgage is selected, the outstanding capital balance will not reduce at all over the 15 years. This means that interest rate changes will change Geoffrey's repayment amount. Most fixed interest rate products are only available for short periods (typically up to five years), which means that Geoffrey is exposed to interest rate risk. Therefore, if Geoffrey were to opt for the endowment mortgage it might not be a bad idea to also take steps to repay some of the debt on a periodic basis to reduce his risks.

5. Unit trusts are funds that are operated by fund managers (banks, brokers or insurance companies). Investment trusts are companies that specialise in investing in shares in other companies.

    A unit trust does not have shares. An investor who wants to invest in an investment trust has to purchase its shares in the stock market, usually from other investors.

    Unit trusts are open-ended investments. An investor in a unit trust purchases units from the fund manager, increasing the size of the fund. When the investor sells units the fund manager decreases the size of the fund (sells underlying investments). Investment trusts are closed-end. When an investor invests in an investment trust they purchase shares in the company, the value of the underlying investments remains the same. When they sell their shares, another investor purchases them and there is no impact on the underlying investments held by the company.

    The value of a unit trust is directly related to the underlying value of the investments the fund holds. The value of an investment company is influenced by this, but is also influenced by the demand for the investment company's shares in the stock market. For example, if the directors have a good track record, it may be that the market will value the investment company's shares higher than the value of the underlying investments, as equity holders anticipate improvements.

Investment trusts can raise debt to expand the investment portfolio, while unit trusts have less scope to do this.

6. The benefits of investing in collective funds are that an investor is able to get access to a wide range of investments that they may not have been able to invest in, on their own. Collective fund managers typically purchase a wide variety of equity shares, bonds, gilts and commercial property. This means that they hold a diversified portfolio of investments so return is not as risky as it would be if the investor only invested in equity. The investor probably would not have sufficient capital to invest in a commercial property so collective funds open doors to this type of investment.

CHAPTER 9 SOLUTIONS

1. A pension is a steady income that is paid to an individual who is typically retired.

2. A public pension is an inflation-indexed annuity that is paid by the government out of social security payments to people who are retired and who have paid social security for a minimum amount of years throughout their life. This pension is mandatory. Individuals cannot opt out of paying their social security, though they have to claim the pension on retirement.

   A private pension is instigated by the individual. It is not mandatory. It is up to each individual to decide whether they want to have a private pension or not. To encourage people to contribute to a private pension, the government allows a tax deduction for contributions made to the pension scheme throughout the working life of the individual. There are limits on the amount that can be paid in each year. A private pension can be received in three ways, a lump sum, an annuity or a combination of both.

3. A personal pension is set up by an individual with an institution which specialises in providing pension policies. Most insurance companies offer pension schemes.

The individual pays into the pension policy independently from their source of income. Their yearly contribution to the scheme is limited (see the chapter for details). All personal pension schemes are money-purchase schemes. This means that the risk associated with the pension not providing a reasonable source of funds in retirement lies fully with the individual.

The total value of the fund on retirement will depend on the contributions made to the pension provider and how well the fund has performed (this will be linked to the stock-markets and the economy). The pension provider will charge for setting up and administering the pension, these charges are taken from the pension fund. The government provides tax relief on contributions made to personal pension schemes up to certain limits of net relevant earnings (see the chapter for details). The income received from a personal pension scheme is taxable on the pensioner.

Company/occupational pension schemes are set up by employers for the benefit of their employees. Both employees and employers' contribute to the scheme. The employee gets a tax deduction for the amount of pension that they contribute – their income tax and social security payments are less. The company also gets a tax deduction for the pension contributions they pay for the employee. There are two types of company pension scheme: defined contribution and defined benefit. These are discussed in the solution to the next question. The income received from a company pension scheme is taxable on the pensioner.

4. A defined contribution scheme is a money-purchase scheme. This means that the company does not guarantee a minimum pension. Both the company and the employee pay into the scheme. The pension received depends on the performance of the scheme assets and the amount of contribution paid in, net of scheme charges. This type of scheme is regarded as more risky than a defined benefit scheme.

A defined benefit scheme is also known as a final salary scheme or a salary scheme. In this situation the company guarantees the employee a set pension, usually a percentage of the final year salary (or an average of the salary received over a number of years). The percentage paid is usually related to the number of years' service given to the employee. The company absorbs all the risk in this type of scheme – where the pension assets fall below what is required to meet future pension commitments, then the company has to make up the difference from its reserves.

Contributions to both types of scheme are treated the same way for tax purposes. A yearly contribution is tax deductible up to a certain percentage of the employees net relevant earnings (there is an overall ceiling level also – see chapter for details).

5. All annuity pension income (public and private) is taxable on the pensioner. The tax paid will depend on whether the individual is a lower or a higher rate tax payer. Retired individuals do not have to pay social security. If the individual has a private pension and opts to receive a 25% lump sum on retirement, then this lump sum is tax-free. If the individual withdraws over 25% the surplus is taxable at the individuals marginal rate of tax.

6. a) Thomas will pay €/£400 each month into the pension scheme (€/£4,000 + 10%). This means that Thomas will only be taxed on €/£3,600 (€/£4,000 − €/£400). Therefore, the tax relief is given at source.

   b) The total contribution to the pension scheme each month on behalf of Thomas is €/£520 (€/£400 + (€/£4,000 × 3%)).

7. a) Thomas' annual pension can be calculated using the following formula:

$$\frac{\text{Years and days}/365}{80} \times \text{pensionable salary} = \text{Annual pension}$$

$$\frac{22 \text{ plus } 304/365}{80} \times \text{€/£48,000} = \text{€/£13,700}$$

   This equates to a monthly pension of €/£1,141.67 (€/£13,700/12). This is subject to income tax.

b) In addition Thomas will receive a lump sum equal to:
€/£pension $\times$ 3 = €/£lump sum
€/£13,700 $\times$ 3 = €/£41,100

CHAPTER 10 SOLUTIONS

1. The steps an individual might take when they believe they have been given advice negligently include the following:

   Initial contact: Contact the entity who sold the product, explain any concerns and state clearly the remedial action required.

   Formal complaint: If the problem is not resolved, contact the firm in writing with a formal complaint. Include all details and specify the outcome required.

   Ombudsman: When unhappy with the response received from the firm contact the relevant ombudsman (independent complaint scheme that is free of charge for consumers). The ombudsman can recommend a solution, or pay out compensation.

   Courts: When unhappy with the decision of the ombudsman, an individual can appeal their decision in the High Court.

2. *ROI*
   In the ROI the financial services industry is monitored by the Irish Financial Services Regulatory Authority (IFSRA). This entity was established on 1 May 2003 to regulate all the financial services businesses in the ROI and to protect the customers of these firms. The IFRSA is part of the Central Bank and Financial Services Authority of Ireland, and is independent of the government.

   The IFSRA try to ensure that financial service businesses are sound, growing and solvent (this promotes confidence in the sector) and to assist financial service customers to make informed decisions about their financial affairs. Their focus in trying to protect consumers is more on problem prevention. The IFSRA provide information on the costs, risks and benefits of the various financial products and services that are available in the ROI, they also monitor competition in the financial service sector and enforce rules on the financial service firms who sell products to consumers to ensure they the transactions are ethical and in customers best interests. In the ROI there are two ombudsman services for financial products: the Financial Services Ombudsman and the Pensions Ombudsman.

UK

In December 2001 the FSA received its statutory powers under the Financial Services and Markets Act (2000) to regulate the financial services industry in the UK. The Financial Services Authority (FSA) is an independent non-governmental body, which regulates the financial services industry in the UK. All firms that wish to undertake financial service activities have to be registered with the FSA. It is a criminal offence to give advice without being authorised by the FSA. Financial advisers must demonstrate competence, honesty and be financially sound. If a financial adviser is called 'independent' they must advise across a range of providers (depolarisation).

The FSA has three strategic aims: to promote efficient and orderly markets; to help financial service consumers achieve a fair deal; and to improve its own business capability and effectiveness. To assist individuals the FSA provides information on all the financial products that are available in the UK and will also provide advice/guidance when an individual considers that they have been treated negligently by their financial adviser. In the UK the Ombudsman is the Financial Ombudsman Service (FOS). This ombudsman will solve help solve disputes between customers and regulated firms. The FSA requires that all financial advisers have professional indemnity insurance. This will meet any compensation claim from customers. When it does not the Financial Services Compensation Scheme (FSCS) can investigate and pay compensation (this is only available to those entities that are regulated by the FSA and may be limited).

ABBREVIATIONS

APR	Annual Percentage Rate
AVCs	Additional Voluntary Contributions
CARE	Career Averaged Re-Valued Earnings
Chng	Price change in the last 24 hours
DSFA	Department of Social and Family Affairs
DINKs	Double Income No Kids
DIRT	Deposit Interest Retention Tax
EAR	Equivalent Annual Return
FSA	Financial Services Authority
FSCS	Financial Services Compensation Scheme
FSO	Financial Services Ombudsman
IFSRA	Irish Financial Services Regulatory Authority
ISA	Individual Savings Account
NI	Northern Ireland
NIC	National Insurance Contributions
P/E	Price Earnings Ratio
PHI	Permanent Health Insurance
PMI	Private Medical Insurance
PPI	Payment Protection Insurance
PRSA	Personal Retirement Savings Accounts
PRSI	Pay Related Social Insurance
ROI	Republic of Ireland
RPI	Retail Price Index
SERPS	State Earnings Related Pension Scheme
SIB	Savings and Investment Board
SSIA	Special Savings Incentive Accounts
SSP	Statutory Sick Pay
S2P	Second State Pension
TESSA	Tax Exempt Special Savings Account
TRS	Tax Relief at Source
UK	United Kingdom
US	United States

VAT	Value Added Tax
Vol.	Volume of transactions
xd	Share Price Ex-Dividend
Yld.	Dividend Yield

BIBLIOGRAPHY

Bawden, A., (2002), Personal Finance: Tangible Assets with less of a Sting Attached, FT.com site.

Department of Social and Family Affairs, (2007), SW 19 'Payments for Retired or Older People, DSFA

Department of Social and Family Affairs, (2007), SW 116 'State Pension (Non-Contributory), DSFA

Department of Social and Family Affairs, (2007), SW 118 'State Pension (Transition) and State Pension (Contributory), DSFA

Directgov.com, (2008), Money, Tax and Benefits, accessed 16 January 2008, http://direct.gov.uk/en/MoneyTaxAndBenefits/

Financial Services Authority, (2007), FSA Fact sheet: The Second State Pension – should you be contracted out?, FSA, London.

Glennon, D., (2008), Investment Outlook 2008, Business Matters: A Newsletter for Chartered Accountants in Business, February 2008 edition.

Harrison, D., (2005), Personal Financial Planning: Theory and Practice, FT Prentice Hall, England.

Heartwood, (2006), Fine Wine –liquid gold?, Horizons, Winter 2006, page 5, www.heartwoodwealth.com

Irish Life Website, (2008), Pensions and PRSA, accessed 16 January 2008, http://www.irishlife.ie/pensions/prsa/employer.html

Ivory, J., (2007), Hugh Grant Sells Warhol Portrait of Elizabeth Taylor, efluxmedia website, 14 November 2007, http://www.eflucmedia.com, accessed 26 March 2008

Redhead, K., (2003), Introducing Investments: A Personal Finance Approach, FT Prentice Hall, England.